Your Complete Guide to Enjoying Wine

Millions of people the world over drink wine as casually as we drink coffee or soda. Yet many Americans still assume that wine drinking is a complicated ritual, requiring specialized knowledge and elaborate equipment. Since all the equipment you really need is a corkscrew and a glass, serving wine at dinner should be as simple as pouring a glass of beer—and it's a lot more fun.

THE SIGNET BOOK OF WINE is your complete guide to enjoying wines. It gives you the basic knowledge you need for developing your own personal preferences, and it serves as a handy reference source for any questions you may have about wine. As sensible in approach as it is comprehensive in outlook, THE SIGNET BOOK OF WINE is a four-star introduction to one of life's greatest pleasures.

"THE SIGNET BOOK OF WINE seems to me to fill a long-felt need for a paperback guide that is informative and accurate. This eminent authority has condensed the lore of wine into a fascinating volume that contains the answers to a tremendous number of questions about wines."

—James Beard

"The best introduction to wine I've ever read . . . as sensibly written as it is comprehensive."

—Charles Monaghan, Editor, *Book World*

"A 'BASIC' BOOK ON WINE THAT THE NOVICE CAN ACTUALLY UNDERSTAND"

THE SIGNET BOOK OF WINE ". . . is a pleasure to recommend. It is written with clarity, charity and understanding for those who may want to know more about wine without having gone beyond a gallon of Gallo. "The introduction to THE SIGNET BOOK OF WINE is an informal, common sense, dissertation on the approach to the testing of wine with the goal of a respectable understanding of what it's all about. It deals with such basics as reading wine labels, fascinating statistics on drinking habits in various countries, and the various types of wine that exist."

—Craig Claiborne, *The New York Times*

"THE SIGNET BOOK OF WINE seems to me to fill a long-felt need for a paperback guide that is informative and accurate. This eminent authority has condensed the lore of wine into a fascinating volume that contains the answers to a tremendous number of questions about wines."

—James Beard

"The best introduction to wine I've ever read . . . as sensibly written as it is comprehensive."
—Charles Monaghan, Editor, *Book World*

The
SIGNET BOOK *of*
WINE

A COMPLETE
INTRODUCTION

Alexis Bespalof

A SIGNET BOOK from
NEW AMERICAN LIBRARY
TIMES MIRROR

Copyright © 1971 by Alexis Bespaloff

SIGNET TRADEMARK REG. U.S. PAT. OFF. AND FOREIGN COUNTRIES
REGISTERED TRADEMARK——MARCA REGISTRADA
HECHO EN CHICAGO, U.S.A.

SIGNET, SIGNET CLASSICS, MENTOR, PLUME AND MERIDIAN BOOKS
are published by The New American Library, Inc.,
1301 Avenue of the Americas, New York, New York 10019

FIRST PRINTING, APRIL, 1971

12 13 14 15 16 17 18 19

CONTENTS

MAPS

ILLUSTRATIONS

Introduction

AMERICA is not a wine-drinking nation. In France, Italy, Spain, and Portugal, for example, wine is taken for granted as the daily beverage of its citizens. In America, the most popular beverage is milk, followed by soda and beer. The annual consumption of wine in France and Italy is more than 200 bottles per person; the average American drinks two bottles a year of table wine. Nor is America a major wine-producing nation; it has an annual production that amounts to less than 3 percent of the world's total. Argentina makes three times as much wine as we do, Russia twice as much.

We simply lack a tradition that would permit us to take for granted a bottle of wine on the dinner table, and to regard wine drinking as one of life's most enjoyable casual pleasures. Whatever start had been made in the production and consumption of wine in this country was cut short by Prohibition, which decreed, in effect, that it was a criminal offense to buy a glass of red wine with your steak, or to serve a guest a bottle of Château Lafite-Rothschild 1900. We have had to make a second start in the past forty years, both as wine producers and as wine consumers, and we have gone about it with great enthusiasm. Consumption of all wines has more than doubled in the past ten years, and the quality of American wines—excellent today—keeps getting better every year.

Despite our late start and the fact that wine is so often thought of as something special and out of the ordinary, there is a greater variety of the world's best wines to be found in almost any American city than in Paris, London, or Rome, and any good wine shop will display more different French wines than you could find in Bordeaux or in Dijon, the capital of Burgundy. Wines of all kinds are readily accessible in almost every state, and an interested

American's approach to wine is much more adventurous than that of the average European. Most Frenchmen, for example, are familiar only with wines from their own part of the country and tend to be condescending about wines from other regions, not to mention wines from other countries. When I lived in Bordeaux I chatted from time to time with the *sommelier,* or wine steward, at one of the city's finest restaurants. He was familiar with all the great châteaux of Bordeaux, and in fifteen years on the job had tasted hundreds of wines in any number of different vintages. In all that time, he had never tasted a Beaujolais or a Chablis: those wines come from the other side of France, and as a Bordelais he had never had the curiosity to try them. Similarly, in the Burgundian village of Pommard, a top wine-maker may have tasted a bottle of Meursault, produced three miles away, the year before last on the occasion of his sister's wedding anniversary.

By comparison, an American who drinks wine even occasionally will probably have tasted some of the following: a Chianti or Valpolicella from Italy; a Beaujolais, Chablis, Châteauneuf-du-Pape, or regional Bordeaux from France; a Portuguese rosé; and a Liebfraumilch or Bernkasteler Riesling from Germany, as well as several wines from California. Because many of the best wines from the world's most famous viticultural regions find their way here, we tend to be more receptive to a variety of wines and more willing to learn than the people who produced them.

Because wine is not treated casually in this country, there are those who go to the other extreme and create a mystique out of drinking a glass of wine. These wine snobs tend to discourage those who come into contact with them, and many people who would enjoy wine have been led to believe that you must know a great deal both about wine and its proper presentation even before you begin. The fear of doing something incorrect has surely kept many people from taking their first steps in wine. In Europe there is no fuss made about drinking wines, just as no one here makes a fuss about drinking coffee. A few Europeans may look into wine more deeply as a hobby, just as there are some Americans who buy fresh coffee beans and grind them to their own specifications. That's no reason for the rest of us to hesitate before drinking a cup of coffee. The only equipment you need to drink wine is a corkscrew and a glass. Two glasses would be better, as one of the most agreeable aspects of wine is that it seems to taste better when shared.

There are people who will tell you that good wines don't travel, or that the best wines can be found only where they are made. It may be true that a wine that tasted superb when drunk on a terrace in a seacoast village in the south of France will not taste as well over here, but in this case it's probably the view that doesn't travel. If a wine can not travel, it is because it doesn't have enough alcohol to stabilize it for a long journey, but this applies almost invariably to the pleasant wines that are served in carafes in holiday resorts. To vinify them so as to increase their alcoholic content by the necessary degree or two would be to deprive them of their charm, and in any case these wines are usually undistinguished in the first place. Someone on holiday is not the most critical and objective of tasters, especially if he does not normally drink wine with his meals at home. There are, it is true, some delightful country wines that are not often seen here, but the reason is that they are not produced in sufficient quantity to make it commercially worthwhile to export them, and they are usually consumed in their entirety within the region where they are made.

The fact of the matter is that all good, soundly made wines can travel, and they do. The best wines in the world can be found here, and they will taste every bit as good as on their home ground. As a matter of fact, the fine wines that are most difficult to find in this country are certain premium varietal wines of California, which are made in limited quantities and rationed out to a few customers.

Wine can be broadly classified into three main groups: table wines, fortified wines, and sparkling wines. *Sparkling wines* obviously include Champagne and various other sparkling and bubbling Champagne-type wines made in most countries in various ways. Sparkling wines are specially taxed in this country, both by the federal government and individually by most states, which accounts for their comparatively high price.

Fortified wines are those to which alcohol has been

added at some point in their production, and they generally contain between 17 and 21 percent alcohol by volume. Wines thus fortified include Sherry, Port, Madeira, and Marsala. Vermouth and various aperitif wines are both fortified and flavored with herbs. Fortified wines, which range in taste from very dry to very sweet, are served before or after a meal and can be enjoyed any time during the day. They are not normally served with a meal.

The term *table wines* properly refers to all wines that contain 14 percent or less of alcohol, and thus includes every kind of natural (unfortified), still (not sparkling) wine that might be served with meals. It is with table wines that this book is primarily concerned, although chapters on both fortified and sparkling wines are included. A few pages also describe brandy, which is distilled from wine.

It may be appropriate here to mention some terms that often crop up in wine discussions. People will occasionally refer to a moderately priced imported wine as a *vin ordinaire,* to distinguish it, perhaps, from the very greatest wines. Actually, *vin ordinaire* more correctly describes the cheap, agreeable, undistinguished wines of anonymous origins that are drunk every day by most Europeans. The wines that are exported to this country are almost always of a higher class, from specific districts: the kind of wine that the citizen of that country might bring out for his Sunday dinner. The closest thing we have to *vin ordinaire* here would be the inexpensive gallon and half-gallon jugs from California that provide pleasant wine at a good price. It's obviously just as inaccurate to refer to an inexpensive wine as "just a table wine," as both a dollar bottle of red wine and Château Haut-Brion 1964 are "just table wines."

The term *vin du pays,* wine of the country, is usually applied to lesser-known wines from particular wine districts which have not achieved much fame, most often because their limited production is consumed locally. To use this phrase in its broadest sense to refer to the produce of a particular nation is redundant, because all wine comes from someplace.

The only way to learn about wines is to taste them, and there is no substitute for pulling a cork. Go into any store that seems to have a reasonably large selection of wines, buy a few different bottles, and then try them one after the other. Even if you come across a wine you don't care for, you will have added to your knowledge without having spent much money. A bottle of wine costs less than a ticket to a new movie these days, and you don't have to stand in line to enjoy it. You can also buy a selection of half bottles, each of which actually contains less alcohol than a cocktail. (A flexible beginning wine cellar is described on page 175.)

Never buy the cheapest wine in any category, as its taste may discourage you from going on. The glass, corks, cartons, and labor are about the same for any wine, as are the ocean freight and taxes for imported wines (which are based on total gallonage, not on value).* Consequently if you spend a little more, you are buying better wine, because the other costs remain fixed. Cheap wines will always be too expensive.

When you eat in a restaurant, try a glass of the bar wine with your meal instead of coffee. It won't be anything special, usually just a gallon jug of inexpensive California wine, but it will be agreeable, and you'll see how pleasant and uncomplicated it is to accompany food with wine. If you particularly enjoyed the bar wine (or if you didn't), ask the bartender to show you the label on your way out, so you'll know what you drank.

Learn to trust your own palate and to determine your own preferences by tasting, not by responding to a label. The other side of this rule is not to assume that what you like, at first, is either very good or, more important, very good value. Only as you expose yourself to different wines will you begin to understand what you like and why. You will also realize what makes one wine better than another, and you will recognize the complexity of taste that characterizes the finest wines.

To learn even a minimum amount about wine you must do two simple things: take a moment to really taste the wine in front of you, and look at the label to determine

---

* Federal taxes and U.S. customs duties on wine are fairly low, and amount to about $1.25 per case of twelve bottles. State taxes vary from as low as 2¢ per case in California, to 23¢ in New York and New Jersey, to more than $2.00 in a few states.

just what it is you are tasting. Tasting is discussed in another chapter, but here are some general guidelines to reading labels quickly.

READING WINE LABELS

The most important fact to remember about wine labels is that most wine names are place-names, and that you are therefore being told, most of the time, just where the wine comes from. Chablis, Sauternes, Pommard, Piesport, Valpolicella, Barolo, Tokay, Châteauneuf-du-Pape, Bernkastel, and Saint-Emilion are all names of individual villages; Beaujolais, Rioja, and Chianti are specific districts in France, Spain, and Italy, respectively. The concept of identification by place of origin is quite different from the one we are most used to—identification by brand name—but it is not unique to wine: we buy Idaho potatoes, Long Island ducklings, Cape Cod oysters, and so on.

Evidently, the characteristics of a wine are closely allied to the soil that produced it, and there has always been an intimate connection between wine and geography. Wherever man has settled, vines have been planted, and grapes crushed to make wine. Wine making developed at different times in different places: grapes have been grown in Italy for 3,000 years, the vineyards of Burgundy were famous in the twelfth century, and commercial wine making in California and Australia began less than 150 years ago. Over the centuries the same basic conclusions were reached, however, in different viticultural regions. We now know, for example, that the vine flourishes best in the temperate zones north and south of the equator: very cold winters kill the vine, and in tropical climates the vine can not complete its natural cycle of growth. Perhaps the most important realization that resulted from trial and error in each region is that certain specific grape varieties are best suited for certain soils, and these are the ones that will produce the finest wines. Some classic combinations of grape and soil include the Cabernet Sauvignon in Bordeaux, the Pinot Noir and Chardonnay in Burgundy, the Nebbiolo in northern Italy, and the Riesling along the Rhine and Moselle.

Quantity and quality have always been mutually exclusive, and the most fertile soils, producing the greatest quantities of grapes, are rarely noted for the quality of their wines. A great vineyard in Bordeaux or Burgundy can produce about 150 cases of twelve bottles each per acre; fertile districts in the south of France or in central California are capable of producing 1,000 cases of undistinguished wine from an acre of vines.

All these considerations were kept in mind when wine laws began to be established in Europe at the beginning of the century. These laws, notably the *appellation contrôlée* laws of France, have been refined to protect the consumer by guaranteeing, with more or less legal force, that the label on a bottle is a true indication of where the wine comes from. These laws take into consideration not only the geographical origin of the wine but also the way it is made, its alcoholic content, the grape varieties used, the quantity produced per acre, and other elements of production that affect quality.

It should be noted that, in a general sense, wine labels are more or less explicit in direct proportion to the quality of the wine contained in the bottle. Labels of lesser wines are not always clear about their geographical origins but, as the quality improves, a label may indicate a region, an inner district within that region, or the ultimate geographical pinpoint, the name of a specific vineyard. Some world-famous vineyards are less than 5 acres in size, others extend for 150 or 200 acres. Although it is standard wine humor to satirize the taster who tries to guess whether a wine comes from the right slope or the left slope, the fact is that the exact position of a plot of vines will have a recognizable effect on the quality of its wines year after year. A vineyard's exposure to the sun, its ability to absorb heavy rains without flooding, the elements in its subsoil that nourish its vines, all these factors and more account for the astonishing fact that the wines of one plot will consistently sell for two or three times as much as those of an adjoining plot.

When you taste a wine, the important thing to remember is not what the label looks like—there are too many to remember them all—but rather what it tells you about the exact origin of the wine you have in your glass. Even when you drink a wine from a specific vineyard, it is more useful at first to determine the district in which the vineyard is

located, such as Saint-Emilion, Burgundy, or the Rheingau, rather than trying to memorize the vineyard name
itself.

There are, of course, exceptions to the general rule that
wines are labeled with their place of origin. Some wines
are identified by a combination of the village name and that
of the particular grape from which it is made: Bernkasteler
Riesling, Cabernet de Maribor. Sometimes wines of a particular region are labeled simply with the grape name alone,
as in Alsace and northern California. This method is
usually adopted in areas whose individual villages or vineyards are not widely known or clearly established.

There also exist some popular fantasy names, which are
often more picturesque than geographically specific. Lacrima Christi, or Tears of Christ, is an Italian wine that
can come from several places, and Liebfraumilch, or Milk
of the Blessed Mother, can be used for just about any wine
from the Rhine Valley.

You should also be aware of the use of generic names,
that is, of a specific place-name that is so well-known to
the public that it has been adopted to describe a type of
wine from somewhere else. California Chablis, Spanish
Burgundy, Chilean Sauternes, and Australian Moselle are
some examples of wines whose names have no relation to
their origin, and whose characteristics may be similar only
in the vaguest way to the wines whose names are being
usurped. The better wines produced in these countries bear
the name of the grape variety from which they are made
or the district from which they come, which gives the consumer a much more accurate idea of what the wine will
actually taste like.

HOW WINE IS MADE

Wine is commonly defined as the fermented juice of fresh
grapes. This obviously leaves out such specialty products
as cherry wine, dandelion wine, or a beverage made from
dehydrated grapes to which water has been added.

Grape juice is transformed into wine by the process of
fermentation, in which the natural sugar present in grapes
is converted into equal parts of alcohol and carbon dioxide

gas. The normal sequence in the making of red wines is for the grapes to be brought to the vinification shed or winery, stripped of their stalks, lightly crushed to release their juice, and put into the fermentation vats. The vats may be open wooden containers, stainless steel cylinders, or enormous glass-lined cement tanks. Where commercially possible, the traditional wooden vats are being replaced by vitreous-lined or stainless steel tanks, which are cleaner and which permit the temperature of the fermenting juice to be more carefully controlled. In Bordeaux, for example, such famous vineyards as Château Latour and Château Haut-Brion now use stainless steel tanks for fermentation. Incidentally, the process of stamping on the grapes by foot (which is pretty rare these days) was carried out not to press the grapes, but to crush them so that the released juice could begin to ferment. Effective presses have been in existence since primitive times, and stamping on grapes would be a pretty ineffective way of getting all the juice out of them.

The juice now begins to ferment as a result of various chemical transformations effected by yeast cells that were already present on the grape skins. (In some regions where very modern techniques are used, the natural yeasts are killed, and special strains of cultured yeasts added to the juice.) As the sugar/water solution becomes an alcohol/water solution (with carbon dioxide gas escaping into the atmosphere) coloring matter and tannin are absorbed from the skins. The amount of color and tannin that are desired determines the length of time that the juice will be in contact with the skins, and this vatting, or *cuvaison*, may vary from two or three days to two or three weeks. With very few exceptions, grape juice is clear and untinted. When a white wine is made from black grapes, as in Champagne, the grapes are pressed immediately, before the skins can impart any undesirable color to the juice. Rosés are traditionally made by keeping the juice and skins together just long enough to impart the right color to the evolving wine, although cheap rosés are sometimes made by mixing red and white wines.

Fermentation normally continues until all of the sugar is converted into alcohol. The resulting wine varies in alcoholic content from 9 to 14 percent or a bit more, depending on the wine region and the nature of the vintage. Even if the juice is especially rich in sugar, an alcoholic content of 14 percent will kill the yeast cells that produced it, and this is why a natural table wine is defined as one with a maximum alcoholic content of 14 percent. The wine is then transferred to small barrels or large tanks to age and to rid itself of its natural impurities. Depending on local custom, aging can take anywhere from a few weeks to three years or more.

Because the ferments are naturally present on grape skins at harvest time, wine making is a natural process, but it must nevertheless be controlled very carefully at every step. If the fermenting juice, called must, gets too cold (an early frost in Germany) or too hot (a late summer in Spain), fermentation will stop and is extremely difficult to start again. What's more, if the new wine were just left exposed to air in its fermentation vat, another natural process would soon take place—through the presence of the vinegar bacteria—which would transform the wine into an acetic acid solution, i.e., into *vin aigre* or sour wine.

With very few exceptions, red table wines are "fermented out" dry, until there is no more than a minute trace of sugar left in the wine. Thus red table wines are technically dry, and what makes one red wine taste "drier" than another is the amount of tannin or acids present.

White wines are made in a slightly different manner. Because they do not need to pick up color from their skins, the grapes are pressed immediately, and the juice ferments away from the skins. As a result, white wines have less tannin than reds, as tannin is derived primarily from the skins. Tannin is an important constituent of fine red wines and gives young wines an astringent, puckerish taste. Its comparative absence from white wines constitutes the principal taste difference between red and white wines.

There are certain naturally sweet white wines, notably Sauternes and Barsac from Bordeaux, and the Spätlese and Auslese wines of Germany, which are the result of fermentation having ended, or having been stopped, while residual sugar remains in the wine.

Besides normal alcoholic fermentation, many wines also undergo *malolactic fermentation,* by which malic acid is converted into lactic acid with carbon dioxide gas as a by-product. This process is of interest to the wine-maker because it decreases the acidity in a wine. It is also of interest to the consumer because if malolactic fermentation takes place after the wine is bottled, the carbon dioxide gas will be trapped in the wine. The resulting delicate sparkle, more noticeable to the tongue than to the eye, is undesirable in a red wine, but can be delightful in certain white wines. Neuchâtel from Switzerland and Vinho Verde from Portugal are enhanced by the effect of malolactic fermentation.

One element of wine making that is often referred to, and which can affect the quality of wines, is *chaptalization*. The word comes from the name Chaptal, the man who first developed the idea of adding natural sugar or sugar and water to the must during fermentation. After a cold or rainy summer, grapes will not have ripened sufficiently, and the resulting lack of natural sugar will produce a wine without enough alcohol to make it healthy and stable. Wine laws vary from country to country and from district to district, but in general chaptalization is permitted in order to raise the alcoholic content of the wine to its normal level as determined by good vintages. Chaptalization can be overdone, but without it many famous wine districts would be unable to produce much drinkable wine in certain years.

At some point before a wine is bottled it is fined, to remove any impurities that may be suspended in it. A primitive form of fining is used by campers when they throw crushed eggshells into coffee that has been made by boiling water and coffee together in a pot. Suspended coffee grounds will cling to the shells as they fall to the bottom of the pot, and as a matter of fact one of the earliest fining methods was to mix beaten egg whites into wine. Nowadays, gelatine and certain clays are widely used. The purpose of fining is to clarify a wine and polish its flavor, although excessive fining will strip a wine of its character.

As wines are bottled, they are filtered to remove any remaining impurities. In the case of inexpensive wines, flash pasteurization is often used. This brief exposure to heat will kill any bacteria that may affect the wine after it has been bottled. Unfortunately, pasteurization effectively stops a wine from developing its qualities in bottle, and it is never used for fine wines. An alternative to pasteurization that has been adopted by some major wineries in this country and certain shippers in Europe is the use of an extremely fine filter that removes the same bacteria that pasteurization would have killed. The result is a clean wine, which will not have the cooked taste that pasteurization can impart.

Wine continues to age after it has been bottled, as the various alcohols, acids, tannins, and other elements present in minute quantities combine and alter the characteristics of the wine. Age alone is no guarantee of quality, however, and it is only the best wines that are sturdy and complex enough to continue to mature for several years. The life cycle of each wine is different, and some wines are at their best when they are bottled, or anyway within six months. Rosés and white wines (except those of the highest class) are best consumed within three years or so of the vintage, as are light red wines. Conversely, the best reds from Bordeaux, Burgundy, northern Italy, Rioja, and California will only begin to show their qualities after four or five years, and it is by no means unusual to discover that a red wine from a top vineyard is only coming into its own after fifteen or twenty years in the bottle.

A note about bottle sizes: fine wines develop more slowly and therefore more completely in larger bottles. For that reason connoisseurs ideally prefer to serve an old red wine from a magnum, which holds two bottles. Naturally, we buy most of our wines in bottles that usually contain twenty-four ounces. Half bottles provide the opportunity of experimenting at less expense. Just remember that a wine will age more quickly in a half bottle, and that a fine wine will never fully develop its qualities in such a small container.

Wine Tasting

FOR A PROFESSIONAL WINE BUYER, wine tasting is a skill requiring a long apprenticeship and rather delicate judgment. For the man who enjoys wine with his meals, tasting is a most enjoyable pastime. But too many people imagine wine tasting to be a complex and mysterious art, dominated by snobs and dilettantes using a stylized and far-fetched vocabulary.

On the simplest level, tasting wines is an inescapable part of drinking them, and there are many people who are content to decide whether a wine is "good" or "not good." Sooner or later the casual wine drinker will experiment with new wines, and at that point he begins to *taste* wine. Unlike most pursuits, such as golf or playing the piano, tasting wines is rewarding from the very start and becomes increasingly fascinating and enjoyable with experience.

The principal difference between the professional taster and everyone else is that he has a better opportunity to taste many different wines, and thus his perspective is wider and his palate more developed. Furthermore, because a buyer tastes wine soon after the vintage, and months or years before the wine is even bottled, he has the additional opportunity of following the development of various wines from the cradle, so to speak. This is especially important as it is his role to judge young wines long before they are ready to be consumed, and he can do this precisely because he has tasted wines of previous vintages at a similar stage of their evolution.

However, there is another aspect of wine tasting that is most important, and that is concentration. We can't all spend days on end going in and out of wine cellars in Burgundy or the Rheingau, but we can at least devote ten seconds or so to a wine when we first taste it with dinner. Different wines and different occasions call for a flexible approach. A bottle of Château Lafite-Rothschild 1953 served at a formal dinner demands more attention (and appreciative remarks) than does a Valpolicella served with pasta. But in each case a few moments' attention to the wine before you is the only way to build your knowledge and increase your pleasure. Look at the label and note where the wine comes from in general terms, and if it's a special wine, note the specific district or vineyard that produced it, as well as the vintage. As you sip the wine, try to place it geographically in your mind, and compare it to other wines you've tasted from the same place. Only in this way will you develop your palate: otherwise you will simply have tasted, in time, a blur of individual bottles that you can neither recall nor repurchase.

It's often assumed, by the way, that "wine experts" are people who can taste wines whose labels have been covered up and name the vineyard and vintage. Although some members of the wine trade amuse themselves by putting their colleagues through such "blind tastings," the real skill of a wine buyer is demonstrated in an exactly opposite manner. He stands in a particular cellar, tasting a specific wine, and has even noted the barrel from which it was drawn. He must now determine how good it is, how good it will be six months or six years later, and what it's worth. It is precisely this ability to concentrate on the wine at hand —in order to judge its value, not guess its origin—which is the primary attribute of his expertise.

When professional tasters are at work, they always spit out the wines they are judging—either onto the floor of a cellar or into a special bucket in a tasting room. For one thing, it's not a pleasant experience to swallow very young red wines starting at eight or nine in the morning. For another, a taster in the vineyard region will sample fifty or seventy-five wines in a day, and if he swallowed each wine, his judgment would soon become impaired, to say the least.

Whatever our specific knowledge about wine, each of us prefers to drink what he likes. As you try different wines, it's interesting to try to determine why one wine is more pleasant than another, what makes the price of one wine three times the price of another, and why one wine might suit a particular dish more than another at the same price: in short, to taste a wine critically and to sort out your impressions. Wine tasters generally approach a wine in three successive steps—color, bouquet (or smell), and taste. These will be examined in some detail, but remember that when it comes to tasting a specific wine, all of these considerations can be reviewed mentally in just a few seconds of concentration.

The first attribute of a wine is its color. Just as we anticipate a dish even more when it's attractively presented on the serving plate, so our enjoyment of a fine wine can be heightened by a look at its color. For this reason, wine is served in clear, uncut glasses. There are two aspects of a wine's color that deserve attention. The first is its appearance in the glass. Whether red or white, a healthy wine should be bright, that is free of any cloudiness or suspension. If a wine appears dull or hazy, it may be unsound in some way, and its unattractive appearance is your first warning signal. This cloudiness is not to be confused with sediment, which is harmless and will fall to the bottom of the glass. Sediment is a natural by-product of age, and older red wines should be decanted whenever possible (as described on page 182). Very occasionally you will come across crystals in a white wine; these are harmless (although admittedly unattractive) tartrates that have been precipitated by excessive cold.

The second aspect of color is the actual hue of the wine. Moselles are pale gold with a touch of green, white Burgundies a richer gold, Beaujolais purple-red, and so on. It happens that red wines get lighter as they age, and white wines get darker. Thus a fine old Bordeaux will be pale brick-red in hue, and an older white wine will take on a deeper gold. This change in color is a good indication of how well—or how badly—the wine is aging. A 1969 Bordeaux that is already pale red, or a young white wine that has taken on a brownish tinge, would immediately be suspect. To judge the hue of a wine, don't look into the glass, as the depth of wine in the glass will affect its color. Tip the glass to one side and look at the outer edge of the wine against a white cloth or backdrop. An indication of just how important color is in judging wines is evidenced by the shape of the traditional Burgundian *tastevin,* used to taste new wines still in wood. It is a shallow silver cup—often used as a decorative ashtray here—with dimpled sides.

Those dimples are there specifically to refract light through the wine, so that its color and appearance can be closely examined.

The second step in judging wine is to smell it, and wine glasses are tapered to focus and retain a wine's bouquet. You may ask, Why bother to smell a wine when I'm about to taste it? About 80 percent of what we imagine to be taste is actually based on our sense of smell. When we taste a roast beef or a peach, it is in fact the olfactory nerves that are doing most of the work. You know that when you have a head cold, you can't taste a thing, and yet it's your nose, not your palate, that is affected by the cold. The reason that wine glasses should be big (at least eight ounces) is that they are meant to be filled only halfway, so that a wine can easily be swirled in the glass. It is this swirling that more fully exposes wine to air, and thus releases the wine's bouquet through evaporation.

A wine's bouquet gives you a strong first impression of the wine itself, and if a wine has any serious faults, they can be discerned by smell, and you can avoid the unpleasantness of tasting bad wine. Occasionally, a wine may be corky, which is revealed by a pronounced smell of cork, rather than of wine. This occurs much less frequently than many people suppose. When tasting minor or inexpensive wines, you should look primarily for the absence of any faults, as such wines are unlikely to have great virtues. Cheap white wines, for example, often cause an unpleasant prickly sensation in the nose, a sign of an excess of sulfur dioxide, used to stabilize wines. Sometimes a wine that has just been opened will smell musty, and swirling the glass to aerate the wine will usually dissipate this smell. From time to time you may come across a white wine that has a suspiciously brown color and a bouquet reminiscent of Sherry, without any of the fruit of a good wine. Such a wine is described as maderized (*maderisé*), because it has the inappropriate smell of Madeira or of Sherry. Maderization is the result of excessive oxidation, and it may have been caused by overlong aging in wood, a faulty cork that let air into the bottle, or it may be the natural evolution of a white wine that is just too old. Another warning signal is a sour, vinegary smell, which indicates that the wine contains an excess of acetic acid, the vinegar acid. If you have ever left out a glass of red wine overnight, what you smell and taste the next day is just such an excess of acetic acid.

When tasting better wines, especially those made from one of the classic grape varieties, you should look for a bouquet that is typical of the wine's origins. A Moselle will be flowery and fragrant, a Beaujolais will also have quite a bit of fruit to it, a red Bordeaux or California Cabernet Sauvignon will have a deeper, more complex bouquet. In general, young wines have more fruit in their bouquet (more of the smell of the grape), while older wines exhibit a more refined and subtle character. The sense of smell is probably the most evocative of all the senses (as the perfume manufacturers discovered long ago), and many of us have a greater sense memory for smells than for taste, so make the most of it.

Finally, you taste the wine. (Remember that judging a wine takes less time than reading about it. Your impressions of color and bouquet should have taken you only a few moments.) The tongue is covered with taste buds that can distinguish only salt, sour, bitter, and sweet, and they are located on different parts of the tongue. You must let the wine rest on your tongue for a moment, so that you can separate the different taste sensations. At this point professional tasters will "whistle in," drawing air into their mouths and through the wine, to help release its flavor. This slurping sound is an accepted part of serious tastings, but it can be dispensed with at dinner parties.

Although there are certain chemical salts in wine, picked up from the soil in which the vines are planted, they are rarely discernible to the taste. Sweetness will, of course, be evident in wines in which residual sugars remain, such as Sauternes, wines from the Rhine, and some rosés. Fine red wines are invariably vinified so as to retain no sugar, and if a Beaujolais or other red wine seems sweet, it may simply denote the presence of glycerin or other elements that round out a wine and give it a certain richness. Some inexpensive California red wines, however, are produced so as to have a trace of sweetness. It's worth noting that not everyone's palate reacts the same way to sweetness: if you take four spoonfuls of sugar with your coffee, you may not really want "a nice dry wine."

Bitterness usually indicates the presence of tannin in wine. Tannin—perhaps the most important component of fine red wines—gives wine an astringent, puckerish quality that you will also taste, for example, in very strong tea. Tannin acts as the spine or skeleton of a wine, and its presence enables a wine to "live" in the bottle for years, while it matures. Tannin comes from grape skins, and its presence is a result of the vinification method used. In Beaujolais, where wines are to be drunk early while they retain their freshness, a short vatting (the time the skins are in contact with the juice) is the rule so that relatively little of the astringent tannin enters the wine. In Bordeaux, where red wines of good vintages are expected to last for ten years or more, vatting may take as long as two weeks, and the resulting wine will be harsh and bitter at first, and unpleasant to drink before it is at least five years old. The great change in vinification in vineyards around the world, and especially in France during the past twenty years, is a trend toward shorter vatting, so that red wines can be consumed more quickly by a public that no longer cellars wine away for years of maturation.

This puckerish quality, then, tells you whether or not the wine is ready to drink, and, with experience, you will be able to determine how long a given wine will continue to improve and how long it will stay at its peak. As a wine ages in bottle, the tannin combines chemically with the coloring matter to form a harmless deposit. That is why older red wines are both paler in color and less harsh to the palate.

Acidity is essential to wine and especially to white wines, where it performs the same function (aiding longevity) as does tannin for reds. A certain amount of acidity is always necessary to give a white wine liveliness and a fresh taste. Very hot summers may produce wines with too little acidity, as the sun burns away the natural tartaric and malic acids in the grapes. Such wines tend to be flabby and short-lived. Too little sun results in grapes that are not fully ripe and contain too much acidity. Such wines are green—tart, sour, and unpleasant.

Besides the impression made on your taste buds, you will also get an overall sense of the wine in your mouth. Some wines are light and delicate, such as a Muscadet; others are rather big and full, such as a Châteauneuf-du-Pape. An unattractive wine may strike you as thin, another as too heavy. It is harmony and balance that is desired in wine, whatever its price. An inexpensive wine with no faults and a pleasant taste may be very good value. An expensive wine from a famous vineyard may be bigger and richer and, in many ways, more interesting, but may nevertheless lack the harmony that would have made it a pleasure to drink.

Tasters also speak of the "farewell" of a wine, the lingering impression that wine leaves in your mouth after you swallow. Some tasters even go so far as to actually count the seconds that this flavor remains on the palate, the longer the better.

Let me state again that the only way to learn about wines is to try different bottles and to be aware of what you are drinking. A good way to define your impressions more accurately is to compare two or three wines at a time: have two half bottles for dinner, or invite like-minded friends over for an informal tasting. If you compare a Bordeaux to a Rioja, or a Beaujolais to a Valpolicella, or a Moselle to an Alsatian Riesling—the possibilities are endless—you will soon learn to distinguish between the major wine-producing regions of the world. More important still, you will discover new wines to enjoy, and the best values from each region.

You will soon realize that one of the great pleasures of drinking wines is to talk about them and to compare impressions. Trying to describe the color, bouquet, and taste of a wine is much less difficult when you are talking to someone who has the same wine in his own glass. The vocabulary of wine tasting may seem vague or precious, at first, but you will discover that its terms are fairly specific and easily understood by anyone who has tasted a number of wines. Although professionals may use technical terms to pinpoint certain impressions, a tasting vocabulary need not be complex. A good wine may be described as charming, delicate, subtle, fresh, lively, tender, spicy, deep, robust, complex, balanced, sturdy, clean, rounded, or crisp. An unpleasant wine may be astringent, dull, heavy, harsh, small, thin, hard, ordinary, cloying, or coarse. It's fascinating to realize that although a wine chemist can easily spot a defective wine, he can not distinguish by chemical analysis between, say, an inexpensive but soundly made Bordeaux

Rouge and a wine from one of the great châteaux of the Médoc. He must taste wine to discover its complexity, subtlety, depth of character, and true value.

One habit that will help to clarify your own taste, and will also help your wine buying considerably, is to keep some sort of record of the wines you drink. Hobbyists keep a cellar book, which can be a specially printed volume with room for various entries, or just a loose-leaf notebook. In theory, you should note the name of the wine, its vintage, and any details that help identify it: when and where you bought it and the price; when you drank the bottle and what you thought of it. If you look back at this record every few months, you'll be amazed at the change in your own preferences.

Another way to keep track of what you drink is to soak off the label and record your comments on the back. The simplest method is to keep an itemized bill from the store and to note your remarks in a couple of words alongside of each wine as you drink it, just to separate the wines you enjoyed most from those you found less to your taste.

As to smoking, a great many wine buyers and professional tasters are smokers, and experiments indicate that people who smoke can taste as well as those who don't. Anyone who doesn't smoke, however, is quickly thrown off by smoke in the air, and for that reason it is common courtesy not to smoke during a tasting or when great wines are served.

The Wines of
France

FRANCE is traditionally considered the greatest wine-producing country in the world. Its annual output of nearly
two billion gallons accounts for about 25 percent of the
world's wines. Although France does not always make the
most wine (in many recent years Italy has edged ahead),
the tremendous variety of wines that it produces include the
very best made anywhere in each category. The red wines
of Burgundy and Bordeaux have no peers, nor do the dry
white wines of Burgundy. The sweet dessert wines of Sauternes and Barsac are equalled only by the top German
wines of the Rhine and Moselle. The best sparkling wines
in the world are made in the Champagne district, and the
wines of the Charente region are distilled to make the best
of all brandies—Cognac.

The first French vineyards were planted about twenty-
five hundred years ago near what is now Marseilles, and
viticulture soon spread to the north and the west. There are
now three million acres of vines in France, and of course
the great bulk of the wine produced is undistinguished. This
is the inexpensive *vin ordinaire* that the Frenchman drinks
every day, and which is widely available in every grocery
store, just as milk and soda are here. Only the top 10 to 15
percent of French wines are entitled to the legal protection
of the *appellation contrôlée* laws. French wines account for
about a third of the table wines imported into the United
States, and almost all of this is of *appellation contrôlée*
quality. What we drink, then, is by no means what the
average Frenchman drinks with his lunch and dinner. Many
Americans drink as a matter of course wines that most
Frenchmen have only heard about.

The *appellation contrôlée* laws, established in the 1930s, are the key to understanding French wine labels. The words mean controlled place-name, and they constitute a guarantee by the government that the place-name on the label is in fact just where the wine comes from. When you have a bottle of French wine in front of you, look for the word directly above *appellation contrôlée* or actually between *appellation* and *contrôlée*. This will indicate the origin of the wine. It may be a region (Bordeaux, Côtes du Rhone), a district (Graves, Anjou), a village (Saint-Julien, Pommard), or even an individual vineyard, as is the case in Burgundy (Chambertin, Montrachet). As the place-name becomes increasingly specific, the *appellation contrôlée* laws become increasingly strict, for they legislate not only the actual geographical limits of a particular place-name, but several other quality-control factors as well. Because certain soils are best suited to certain grape varieties, the law specifies which varieties are permitted. Minimum alcoholic content is another factor, not because the best wines have the most alcohol (just about all the French wines we drink contain between 11 and 13 percent), but because too little alcohol in a wine will render it unstable. This prevents the use of an established place-name for all of the wines produced there in a very poor year, when the worst of them will be too thin and washed-out to be typical. Perhaps the most important control of all, however, is that of quantity. It's been observed that most of the world's best wine regions do not, in fact, contain the best or most fertile soil: the vine seems to thrive in difficult terrain. In Bordeaux, for example, the richest soil, known as *palus*, lies along the riverbanks. These strips of land are specifically excluded from being planted in vines to make Bordeaux. Furthermore, the best grape varieties rarely give a high yield, and should not be permitted to overproduce. An individual vine nourishes its fruit by sending roots down into the soil, as does any plant. If the vine is not pruned back in the winter to limit the number of bunches it can produce, the same root will have to nourish a lot more bunches, and the resulting wine will be lacking in depth and character. Good examples of the truth of this observation are the 1945 and 1961 vintages in Bordeaux, when bad weather during the flowering season considerably reduced the num-

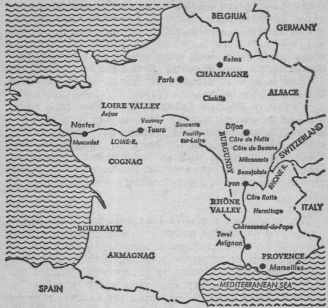

The Wine Regions of France

ber of bunches on each vine. The result of this natural pruning, which was followed by a very hot summer, was a small crop of superb quality. To take a specific example from the *appellation contrôlée* laws for the Bordeaux region, the production of wine entitled to be called Bordeaux is limited to 220 cases per acre; that of a specific village, such as Pauillac, is limited to 176 cases. Similarly, the production of Burgundy is limited to 200 cases per acre; that of a specific Burgundy vineyard, such as Chambertin or Montrachet, cannot exceed 133 cases. Because *appellation contrôlée* laws determine both the exact geographical limits of an appellation and its maximum production per acre, no district can expand its production to meet the increasing worldwide demand. The result has been a significant rise in the price of wines from the best-known areas, especially in the past ten years.

Occasionally, you may see a cheap bottle of French wine whose label bears the name of a specific wine district, usually Bordeaux, as the address of the shipper, but you will look in vain for the words *appellation contrôlée* anywhere on the label. Such wines are known as nonappellation wines, and can, of course, come from anywhere at all.

There is another category of French wines known as V.D.Q.S.—*Vins Délimités de Qualité Supérieure*, or Delimited Wines of Superior Quality. These wines rank below those of *appellation contrôlée* because their quality is not as good or as consistent. The labels of V.D.Q.S. wines, among which are Côtes de Provence, Béarn, and Corbières, are imprinted with an emblem that looks like a postage stamp, and which contains the appropriate words plus an illustration of a hand holding a wine glass.

The *appellation contrôlée* laws were based on earlier attempts to control the authenticity and quality of French wines, which were in turn made necessary by the confusion resulting from the complete replanting of the French vineyards after their destruction by phylloxera toward the end of the nineteenth century. Phylloxera is a plant louse that was unwittingly brought over from the United States on American rootstocks, and which began to infest the European vineyards about one hundred years ago. Various methods were proposed to combat the phylloxera epidemic, which was devastating the vineyards of one country after another, but the technique that finally worked was to graft European *vitis vinifera* vines to native American rootstocks from the eastern United States that were resistant to this insect. Eventually just about every single vine in Europe (and most of those in California) was grafted onto an American rootstock.

BORDEAUX

Bordeaux is the center of the world's fine wines. Within France, Burgundy produces outstanding wines as well, but Bordeaux is unmatched for both quantity and variety. Red, white, and rosé is produced, and the white wines are both dry and sweet. The forty or fifty million cases produced annually in Bordeaux constitute more table wine than is produced in California or, in some years, in all of Germany. Although this amounts to less than 10 percent of the wines of France, Bordeaux accounts for one-third of all wines entitled to *appellation contrôlée* status.

Bordeaux was shipping its wines to England as early as the twelfth century, when Henry II married Eleanor of Aquitaine and thus annexed the region of Bordeaux as part of his empire. At that time, thousands of barrels were shipped annually of a pale red wine called *clairet*. The word evolved into claret, and properly refers only to red wine from Bordeaux, although it is often used in

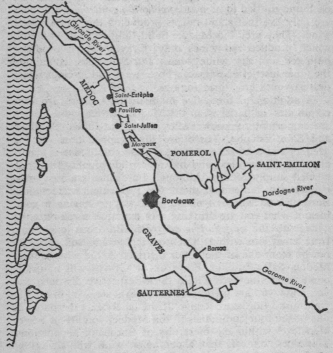

The Bordeaux Districts

other countries to describe any dry red wine. It's only since the early nineteenth century, when the use of corks and bottles became more common, that claret as we know it today began to be produced: a deep-colored red wine that improves with age and that, in fact, needs years in barrel and in bottle to develop its best qualities.

The Bordeaux wine region lies within the *département* (similar to our state) of the Gironde, and its principal city is, of course, Bordeaux itself, with a population of 250,000. Two rivers, the Garonne and the Dordogne, meet just north of Bordeaux and form the Gironde estuary, which flows into the sea. It is in and around this triangle that the vineyards of Bordeaux are located.

There are more than thirty wine districts in Bordeaux, each one entitled to its own *appellation contrôlée,* but there are only five that stand out as producing the very greatest wines. They are: the Médoc, Saint-Emilion, and Pomerol, which produce red wines only; Graves, which produces both red and dry white wines; and Sauternes, containing the inner district of Barsac, whose sweet and luscious white dessert wines are world famous.

In addition to these five main districts, there are four communes, or parishes, in the Médoc district whose names are important to know: Margaux, Saint-Julien, Pauillac, and Saint-Estèphe. These are inner appellations of the Médoc, and a wine from one of these communes is generally of a higher class and has more individuality than one labeled simply Médoc. Although Bordeaux is a vast area, if you can remember these ten place-names (including Barsac), you will be well on your way to having a good idea of what you are drinking. For example, a red or white wine with the *appellation contrôlée* Bordeaux can come from anywhere within the entire region and will certainly not be from one of the better districts. A red wine labeled Médoc, Saint-Emilion, Pomerol, or Graves will naturally come from vineyards within those respective districts, and you know you are getting a wine several steps up in quality from just a Bordeaux Rouge. If the label bears the name of one of the four communes in the Médoc, you are at a very high level within the hierarchy of Bordeaux appellations. This doesn't mean that a commune wine will always be better than a Médoc, but at least this provides a useful and fairly consistent ranking of relative quality.

When you are confronted with the label of an individual vineyard, looking for the *appellation contrôlée* is the simplest way to place it geographically. Let's say you are served a bottle of Château Pétrus, and having enjoyed it, decide to buy a bottle for yourself. You will discover that a wine from this particular vineyard in a good vintage sells for around twenty dollars a bottle, but if you noted its *appellation contrôlée,* you would have seen that it's a Pomerol. The chances are, then, that another Pomerol at a price you care to pay will have more of the general characteristics of Château Pétrus than, say, a Graves or a plain Bordeaux. If you try to memorize a vineyard name or the general appearance of a label, you will just be searching for one label among hundreds, instead of focusing your effort on a particular wine from one of the few major red wine districts.

Knowing these few names is also useful in reverse, that is, if a bottle of Bordeaux bears an unfamiliar *appellation contrôlée,* you know by the process of elimination that it must come from one of the many lesser districts. You may see names such as Côtes de Fronsac, Entre-Deux-Mers, Bourg, Blaye, and the like, and while such wines can be excellent buys and very agreeable wines indeed, you should not expect to pay much more than three dollars for such a bottle.

I have dwelt on the principal Bordeaux appellations because individual vineyards (called châteaux) play a much greater role in the marketing of Bordeaux wines than in those of any other region. The consumer in a well-stocked store will be confronted with a profusion of individual château names, and because of American marketing methods, it is easy to treat these châteaux as so many individual brands. Many wine drinkers seem to limit themselves to the wines of just a few châteaux whose names they remember and hesitate to experiment. In fact, once you know the few important appellations, it's easy enough to try wines of different prices within an appellation, or to compare wines of similar price in different appellations. Anyone who wants to study the wines of Bordeaux in more detail will eventually become familiar with its most important châteaux, which are listed district by district in this chapter.

Although an individual vineyard in Bordeaux is traditionally called a château, there are very few homes that would merit this description. Most properties consist of just a country house, some have more elaborate buildings dating from the late eighteenth or early nineteenth centuries, and a few properties have no more than a large *chai*, or ground-level shed, where the wines are made and stored. Nevertheless, labels for individual Bordeaux vineyards almost all contain the word *château* (a very few describe themselves as *domaine* or *clos*), and while there are a few properties elsewhere in France that also call themselves by a château name, when you see this word on a label, you can be pretty sure that the wine is from Bordeaux.

Although there are more than two thousand individually named properties in Bordeaux, there are no more than perhaps sixty red wines and fifteen or twenty dry and sweet white wines that can readily be found in the better wine stores or on wine lists. One important fact about Bordeaux vineyards that makes learning about them much easier is that it is traditional here for a property to belong to a single owner. Furthermore, all of the wines from a vineyard that are to be sold under the château name are blended together in the January following the vintage, so that each property produces only one wine bearing its name in any one vintage. By contrast, most Burgundy vineyards have several owners, each one making a slightly different wine each year according to his skills and intentions. In Germany, each grower deliberately produces several different wines from the same vineyard in any good vintage, and these will vary considerably in quality, flavor, and price. By comparison with these two other great wine regions, Bordeaux is relatively easy to study, and many connoisseurs can discuss Bordeaux châteaux with great knowledge and enthusiasm, while remaining mystified about the wines of Burgundy or the Rhine.

The reason that there are so many famous châteaux in Bordeaux is because each of them has its own particular and distinct characteristics. It may seem hard to believe, but each parcel of soil will produce a wine that is not only different from parcels nearby, but which is also consistently better or less good than those of its neighbors. A case in point is Château Latour and Château Léoville-Las-Cases: these two vineyards are contiguous, and it is impossible for a visitor to determine, unaided, where one vineyard ends and the other begins. Yet the first is a Pauillac, the second a Saint-Julien, and a bottle of Latour costs two or three times as much as a bottle of the (nevertheless excellent) Léoville-Las-Cases. Although the potential quality of a vineyard is determined by its soil and subsoil, its exposure to the elements and to the sun, there are other factors that enter into the quality and personality of the wine of a particular château. The grape varieties that are permitted for red Bordeaux are primarily the Cabernet Sauvignon, Cabernet Franc, and Merlot, plus small quantities of the Malbec and Petit-Verdot, and for whites the Sémillon and Sauvignon Blanc. The Cabernet Sauvignon brings finesse and depth of flavor to a red wine—the classic qualities of a claret; the Merlot is known for its suppleness and charm. Since the public has been drinking its red Bordeaux sooner and sooner after the vintage, before the wines have fully developed their qualities, a number of vineyards have replanted their acreage with a greater proportion of Merlot than previously. The resulting wine is softer and sooner ready to drink. To achieve a similar goal, another château may decide on a shorter vatting—the time during which the grapes are in contact with the fermenting must—and thus produce a somewhat lighter and quicker-maturing wine. These are just some of the factors that can affect the personality of a wine, and comparing various châteaux in various vintages provides an endless source of pleasure to drinkers of Bordeaux.

Some years ago the best châteaux of Bordeaux began to bottle their wines themselves in their own cellars—rather than shipping them in barrels—as insurance that the wines bearing their labels are in no way tampered with. A branded cork bearing the name of the château and the vintage is used as well. Such wines bear the words *Mis(e) en bouteille(s) au château,* that is, château bottled. Just about every important château wine imported into this country is now château bottled. In recent years, as Americans have learned to look for the words *mis en bouteille au château* on a Bordeaux label, a number of smaller properties have taken to château bottling their wines as well. Wines of these *petits châteaux,* or lesser properties, as they are called, have become very popular here, and are generally available at $1.50 to $3 a bottle. Their quality will vary considerably, and it is well to remember that if a wine is château bottled you are guaranteed of its authenticity, but not necessarily of its quality. It's perfectly possible to bottle a second-rate wine at the property, and this is being done to take advantage of the momentum for château-bottled wines. There are, of course, a number of large, carefully-tended properties in various districts that consistently produce good wines, and it's worth experimenting with the selection of *petits châteaux* available locally.

Another important category of Bordeaux wines is the regional blends made up by the many individual shippers known as *négociants,* and sold simply as Bordeaux, Médoc, Saint-Emilion, Saint-Julien, and so forth. These are made up of wines from many properties within the particular appellation, and this flexibility permits reputable shippers to bottle wines of consistent quality. Such wines, while dependable, are sometimes a bit more expensive than a well-made *petit château,* which may, in turn, have more distinction to it.

The word *monopole* on a shipper's label simply indicates that he has a monopoly, or exclusivity, on the particular brand name that he is using for that wine, which is self-evident. *Grand vin* doesn't have any official meaning either, although *grand crû* does.

Bordeaux Supérieur and Graves Supérieur only means that wines so labeled contain 1 or 2 percent more alcohol than those labeled simply Graves or Bordeaux. It is absolutely no indication of superior quality and in fact many excellent châteaux who could legally add *supérieur* to their appellations don't bother to do it.

The Médoc

The Médoc district contains some of the most famous vineyards in the world, and most of its wines are on a very high level indeed. The wines of the Médoc have become well-known only in the last 150 years or so. The wines shipped to England in the Middle Ages were mostly from

Graves, whose vineyards are just outside the city of Bordeaux. The Médoc, which stretches out sixty miles from Bordeaux, remained a dangerous and unprotected place in which to travel, and it was not until the beginning of the seventeenth century that important vineyards were established there.

The Médoc is actually divided into two parts, originally known as the Haut-Médoc and the Bas-Médoc. These references to high and low have to do only with the relative heights of the terrain, but the proprietors in the Bas-Médoc objected to its possible connotations on a label, and their appellation is now simply Médoc. The famous communes of Saint-Estèphe, Pauillac, Saint-Julien, and Margaux are, in fact, located in the Haut-Médoc, but this district is nevertheless habitually referred to simply as "the Médoc," both on labels and in conversation.

Perhaps the best way to approach the wines of the Médoc is from the top, which is to say, with the Classification of 1855. In conjunction with the Paris Exhibition of that year, representatives of the Bordeaux wine trade were asked to draw up a list of the best vineyards of the Médoc and of Sauternes, which will be discussed separately. By this time the Médoc had become considerably more famous than Graves, and Saint-Emilion and Pomerol were not yet widely known. The resulting classification grouped the wines on five levels of excellence, from *premiers crûs* to *cinquièmes crûs*. (Château Haut-Brion, located in the Graves district, was too important to leave out.) *Crû* means growth, that is, the particular terrain that constitutes an individual vineyard. A fifth growth was by no means only one-fifth as good as a first growth—the ranking was gradual—and in any case al. the classified growths represented the very best that Bordeaux had to offer.

THE CLASSIFICATION OF 1855
FOR THE MÉDOC

Premiers Crûs—First Growths

VINEYARD	COMMUNE
Château Lafite-Rothschild	Pauillac
Château Margaux	Margaux

| Château Latour | Pauillac |
| Château Haut-Brion | Pessac |

Deuxièmes Crûs—Second Growths

Château Mouton-Rothschild	Pauillac
Château Rausan-Ségla	Margaux
Château Rauzan-Gassies	Margaux
Château Léoville-Las-Cases	Saint-Julien
Château Léoville-Poyferré	Saint-Julien
Château Léoville-Barton	Saint-Julien
Château Durfort-Vivens	Margaux
Château Lascombes	Margaux
Château Gruaud-Larose	Saint-Julien
Château Brane-Cantenac	Cantenac-Margaux
Château Pichon-Longueville	Pauillac
Château Pichon-Longueville-Lalande	Pauillac
Château Ducru-Beaucaillou	Saint-Julien
Château Cos d'Estournel	Saint-Estèphe
Château Montrose	Saint-Estèphe

Troisièmes Crûs—Third Growths

Château Kirwan	Cantenac-Margaux
Château d'Issan	Cantenac-Margaux
Château Lagrange	Saint-Julien
Château Langoa-Barton	Saint-Julien
Château Giscours	Labarde-Margaux
Château Malescot-Saint-Exupéry	Margaux
Château Cantenac-Brown	Cantenac-Margaux
Château Palmer	Cantenac-Margaux
Château La Lagune	Ludon
Château Desmirail	Margaux
Château Calon-Ségur	Saint-Estèphe
Château Ferrière	Margaux
Château Marquis-d'Alesme-Becker	Margaux
Château Boyd-Cantenac	Cantenac-Margaux

Quatrièmes Crûs—Fourth Growths

Château Saint-Pierre	Saint-Julien
Château Branaire-Ducru	Saint-Julien
Château Talbot	Saint-Julien
Château Duhart-Milon	Pauillac
Château Pouget	Cantenac-Margaux
Château La Tour-Carnet	Saint-Laurent

Château Lafon-Rochet	Saint-Estèphe
Château Beychevelle	Saint-Julien
Château Prieuré-Lichine	Cantenac-Margaux
Château Marquis-de-Terme	Margaux

Cinquièmes Crûs—Fifth Growths

Château Pontet-Canet	Pauillac
Château Batailley	Pauillac
Château Haut-Batailley	Pauillac
Château Grand-Puy-Lacoste	Pauillac
Château Grand-Puy-Ducasse	Pauillac
Château Lynch-Bages	Pauillac
Château Lynch-Moussas	Pauillac
Château Dauzac	Labarde
Château Mouton-Baron-Philippe*	Pauillac
Château du Tertre	Arsac
Château Haut-Bages-Libéral	Pauillac
Château Pédesclaux	Pauillac
Château Belgrave	Saint-Laurent
Château Camensac	Saint-Laurent
Château Cos Labory	Saint-Estèphe
Château Clerc-Milon-Mondon	Pauillac
Château Croizet-Bages	Pauillac
Château Cantemerle	Macau

* Formerly Château Mouton d'Armailhacq.

Over a hundred years have gone by, but this classification remains unchanged today, and its names and ratings are more or less familiar to all lovers of claret. Most of the wines on the list continue to indicate on their labels that they are a *crû classé* or *grand crû classé,* and any discussion of Bordeaux vineyards will always turn to the classified growths, despite the fact that they account for less than 3 percent of the annual production of Bordeaux. For these reasons, and because it can be a very useful guide to buying Bordeaux, the classification deserves some attention here.

Although the classification remains remarkably valid in many ways, and many of its wines are still among the best produced in Bordeaux, there are some reservations to be made. For one thing, certain châteaux are no longer considered of much interest and their wines are not often seen here. For another, the classification gave such prominence to the châteaux of the Médoc that the excellent vineyards of Graves, Saint-Emilion, and Pomerol were neglected until fairly recently. Perhaps the most interesting development within the classification itself is that there has been so much attention focused on the four first growths, Lafite, Latour, Haut-Brion, and Margaux, that their prices are now two or three times that of any other classified wine: ten to fifteen dollars a bottle for a good recent vintage, and twenty-five dollars or more for vintages such as 1959 or older. To these four must be added Château Mouton-Rothschild, which never accepted its status as first of the seconds, and whose pride has been justified by time: its wines are now as expensive as those of Lafite.

This leads to the important point that the classification was, in fact, based on the prices that each wine had sold for in a number of previous vintages. This pragmatic approach to the value of a property is the one still in use today among the brokers and shippers of Bordeaux. In the Bordeaux wine trade, the wines of the classification are referred to simply as the first growths and the second growths, the latter category including all but the five most expensive wines. Among "the seconds" are a number of wines officially rated as third, fourth, or fifth growths that consistently achieve the same prices as the classified seconds, and in some cases, a bit more. To use the classification effectively, look over the list from time to time so that you will know when you are drinking the wine of one of the more famous châteaux of Bordeaux. What you should not do is to pay undue attention to the exact rating of every wine, because a wine's relative price on a complete list of Bordeaux châteaux will give you a better indication of the way the Bordeaux wine merchants themselves rate the wine today.

There were also a number of other châteaux rated just below the *grands crûs classés* as *crûs exceptionels* and *crûs bourgeois*. Nowadays, the term *crû bourgeois,* or bourgeois growth, is applied to any property that sets high standards for itself and whose wines can be favorably compared to those of the classified growths. Among the many *crûs bourgeois* making excellent wine today are the following:

Château Angludet —	Château La Tour-de-Mons
Château Beau-Site	Château Liversan
Château Bel-Air-Marquis- d'Aligre	Château Loudenne
	Château Marbuzet
Château Capbern	Château Maucaillou
Château Chasse-Spleen	Château Meyney
Château Dutruch Grand Pujeaux	Château Les Ormes de Pez
	Château Paveil de Luze
Château Fourcas-Dupré	Château Peyrabon
Château Fourcas Hostein	Château de Pez
Château Glana	Château Phélan-Ségur
Château Gloria	Château Poujeaux-Theil
Château Greysac	Château Siran
Château Haut Marbuzet	Château du Taillan
Château Labégorce	Château Tronquoy-Lalande
Château Lanessan	Château Verdignan

The wines of the Médoc are known especially for their breed and finesse, and are the most elegant of all the Bordeaux. The greatest châteaux need some years to show their distinctive qualities, and a wine that is still improving after thirty years in the bottle is not exceptional, although finding such a wine is.

One typical way to tour the Médoc is to drive straight out to Saint-Estèphe, the farthest village from Bordeaux, and then to visit the principal properties in turn. There are three châteaux in Saint-Estèphe whose wines are very familiar here—Cos d'Estournel, Montrose, and Calon-Ségur—and many other châteaux are found here as well, as Saint-Estèphe is by far the biggest wine-producing village in the Médoc. Saint-Estèphe wines are quite firm and tannic when young, and develop slowly: they are among the least supple of all clarets.

Pauillac surely has the highest average quality of wine of any village in France. Three great châteaux are located there—Lafite-Rothschild, Latour, and Mouton-Rothschild —as well as a number of other properties whose wines are justifiably popular. Château Lafite-Rothschild is one of the few properties whose house resembles a château, and few sights are more impressive than the first view of its *chai* for the new wine. In a spacious and high-ceilinged ground-level warehouse, a thousand barrels are lined up in several rows, representing perhaps two million dollars' worth of maturing wine. A second wine is also made at the property, Carruades de Château Lafite-Rothschild, which comes entirely from the Lafite vineyard, but is essentially made up of somewhat lighter wines from younger vines.

In the châteaux of Bordeaux, wines are stored in *barriques,* small oak barrels that hold about fifty-five gallons, or twenty-four cases of wine. The red wines remain in barrels for twenty to thirty months at the best properties, and this aging contributes greatly to the complexity, depth of flavor, and distinctive character of fine red wines. (In fact, the best California wineries have been converting from the use of large redwood vats to small oak barrels for the aging of their best red wines for this very reason.) The measure of trade in Bordeaux when new wines are being bought is the *tonneau,* an imaginary measure equivalent to four *barriques,* or ninety-six cases.

Château Mouton-Rothschild is the home of Baron Philippe de Rothschild, who recently established a fascinating wine museum at the property. The labels of this wine are distinguished by the design of a different artist every year, including Henry Moore (1964), Salvador Dali (1958), and Jean Cocteau (1947). The Bordeaux firm that markets Château Mouton-Rothschild also ships a dependable red and white regional Bordeaux called Mouton Cadet.

Château Latour encompasses little more than modest living quarters, apart from its wine *chais,* although the ancient tower that gives the property its name and appears on its label still stands. Stainless steel fermentation *cuves* were installed in time for the 1964 vintage (Château Haut-Brion had already been using similar *cuves),* and these moves by first growths have encouraged other châteaux to adopt more modern methods of wine making. There are many Bordeaux vineyards that have incorporated the name Latour on their labels, but the one great château of this name is this one, in Pauillac.

Château Pichon-Longueville, a second growth of Pauillac, has long been divided into two parts, one labeled

Baron Pichon-Longueville, the other, Comtesse de Lalande. Because the wine is usually listed on restaurant lists simply as Château Pichon-Longueville, some wine buffs like to ask the wine steward if the wine is that of the baron or the countess, to show their expertise. In any case, the wines of the countess are now being labeled simply Château Pichon-Lalande.

Saint-Julien does not have any first growths, but it does have eleven classified châteaux within its borders, just about all of them are available here, and they are excellent wines. Saint-Julien wines are somewhat softer and more supple than those of Saint-Estèphe and Pauillac, and mature more quickly. The three Léovilles are well-known—Châteaux Léoville-Las-Cases, Léoville-Poyferré, and Léoville-Barton —as well as Châteaux Talbot, Gruaud-Larose, and Beychevelle.

Margaux produces wines noted for their elegance and rich texture: they are often described as suave. Château Margaux, a first growth, is its most famous vineyard, and the fact that it bears the same name as the commune itself has often led to confusion. A blend of wines from various properties within the village will simply be called Margaux. But there is only one Château Margaux, and there could only be a general family resemblance between a regional Margaux and the wine of this outstanding property. The wines of the nearby commune of Cantenac are entitled to be sold as Margaux, and usually avail themselves of this better-known appellation. There are a number of excellent classified growths in Margaux, among them Château Lascombes—considerably improved under the supervision of Alexis Lichine—and Château Palmer.

Two excellent classified vineyards that are not situated within the four main communes of the Médoc are Château La Lagune and Château Cantemerle. There are also two other communes—Listrac and Moulis—whose appellations are sometimes seen on château-bottled wines, and they are often well priced.

There is no white Médoc as such, because the appellation applies only to red wines. There is, however, some pleasant white wine made by a few châteaux in the district, and entitled to the *appellation contrôlée* Bordeaux Supérieur.

Graves

The Graves district (whose name is derived from its gravelly soil) begins just at the city limits of Bordeaux, and its most famous vineyard, Château Haut-Brion, can be reached by bus. As a matter of fact, land developers in Bordeaux have already bought up parcels of all but the best vineyards nearest the city and are turning them into housing projects. At one time the red wines of Graves were the most famous of all the Bordeaux, but today the district is known mainly for its inexpensive white wines. A regional wine labeled simply Graves or Graves Supérieures will invariably be white, and it's often assumed that Graves makes only white wines: actually, a third of its production is red. The red wines are usually sold under their individual château names, and are generally of a much higher class than the whites.

White Graves is a dry wine, but not nearly as dry as a Burgundy, and its slightly mellow quality has made the wine less popular than, say, Chablis or Pouilly-Fuissé. Furthermore, it is accepted practice to stabilize white wines with a bit of sulfur dioxide, and nowhere is this more evident than in the bouquet and taste of the cheapest Graves. The château wines are certainly more carefully made and a number of them are distinctive.

It is the red wines from individual châteaux, however, that are of the most interest, and some of them are among the best wines of France. If they lack the finesse of the best Médocs, they have instead a richer texture and are tremendously appealing clarets. Not only is Château Haut-Brion officially rated on a par with the first growths of the Médoc, but two other red Graves, Château La Mission-Haut-Brion and Domaine de Chevalier, consistently sell for more than any second growth of the Médoc.

The wines of Graves were classified in 1953 and again in 1959. Different levels of quality were not set up, as in the Médoc, and all of these wines are rated equally as *crûs classés*, or classified growths. Naturally, Château Haut-Brion is considered to be in a class by itself.

Graves is the only important district in Bordeaux where many classified properties make both red and white wines.

GRAVES

Crûs Classés—Classified Growths

Red Wines

Château Bouscaut
Château Carbonnieux
Domaine de Chevalier
Château de Fieuzal
Château Haut-Bailly
Château Haut-Brion
Château La Mission-Haut-
  Brion

Château La Tour-Haut-Brion
Château Kressmann La Tour*
Château Malartic-Lagravière
Château Olivier
Château Pape Clément
Château Smith-Haut-Lafitte

White Wines

Château Bouscaut
Château Carbonnieux
Domaine de Chevalier
Château Couhins
Château Haut-Brion

Château Kressmann La Tour*
Château Laville-Haut-Brion
Château Malartic-Lagravière
Château Olivier

Other good red and white wines from Graves include:

      Château Baret (RW)
      Château Larrivet Haut-Brion (R)
      Château La Louvière (RW)

* Formerly Château La Tour-Martillac.

Saint-Emilion

The picturesque village of Saint-Emilion is about twenty miles northeast of Bordeaux, and to drive there one must cross both the Dordogne and the Garonne rivers. Saint-Emilion is a medieval village whose winding streets are paved with cobblestones, and one of its main tourist attractions is a monolithic church whose chapel was carved out of a granite hillside a thousand years ago, arches, pillars, and all. The local restaurants feature a dish that visitors are always encouraged to try without necessarily being told what it contains: it is *lamproie*, the local eel, cooked in red wine and one of the few seafood dishes that is traditionally served with a red wine. The worldwide fame of Saint-Emilion, however, is its wine. Vineyards begin at the very edge of town and, unlike those of the Médoc and Graves, are to a large extent planted on slopes rather than flatlands. Saint-Emilion produces almost as much wine as the entire Médoc, and as no inner appellations exist, the name Saint-Emilion is perhaps best known of all the Bordeaux appellations.

Saint-Emilion is often referred to as the Burgundy of Bordeaux because its wines are fuller and rounder than, say, those of the Médoc—the result of somewhat richer soil and a greater proportion of Merlot grapes. This comparison is probably misleading, however, as Saint-Emilions very much exhibit the classic qualities of Bordeaux, although they tend to mature more quickly than the wines of the Médoc and Graves. In 1955 the wines of this district were officially classified into a dozen *premiers grands crûs classés*, and about sixty *grands crûs classés*. A number of other châteaux are entitled to call themselves simply *grands crûs*, so that you have to look carefully at a Saint-Emilion château label to determine its relative standing among the three official levels of *grands crûs*. Two of the *premiers grands crûs* of St. Emilion, Château Cheval Blanc and Château Ausone, are considered on a par with the first growths of the Médoc and are as expensive.

Adjoining Saint-Emilion proper are five small *appellations contrôlées* communes to whose names Saint-Emilion has been affixed. The best known are Saint-Georges-Saint-Emilion and Montagne-Saint-Emilion, and both contain some châteaux whose wines can surpass those of a regional Saint-Emilion.

All of the *premiers grands crûs classés* are listed here, as well as many of the *grands crûs classés* that are available in the United States.

SAINT-EMILION

Premiers Grands Crûs—First Great Growths

Château Ausone	Château Beauséjour-Fagouet
Château Cheval Blanc	Château Belair
Château Beauséjour-Duffau- Lagarrosse	Château Canon Clos Fourtet

Château Figeac
Château La Gaffelière*
Château Magdelaine

Château Pavie
Château Trottevieille

Grands Crûs Classés—Great Classified Growths

Château L'Angélus
Château Balestard-la-Tonnelle
Château Canon-la-Gaffelière
Château Corbin
Château Corbin-Michotte
Château Curé-Bon
Château Dassault
Château Fonroque
Château Grand-Corbin
Clos des Jacobins
Château La Clotte

Château La Dominique
Château Larcis-Ducasse
Château La Tour-du-Pin-
  Figeac
Château Pavie-Macquin
Château Ripeau
Château Soutard
Château Tertre-Daugay
Château Trimoulet
Château Troplong-Mondot
Château Villemaurine

Other St. Emilion châteaux include:

Château Curé-Bon-la-Madeleine
Château La Grâce-Dieu
Château Lapelletrie
Château Simard

* Formerly Château Gaffelière-Naudes

Pomerol

Pomerol is the smallest of the top wine districts of Bordeaux, producing about 15 percent as much wine as Saint-Emilion. Pomerol in fact adjoins the Saint-Emilion district, and for many years its wines were grouped with those of its better-known neighbor. About fifty years ago Pomerol was accorded a standing of its own, and its wines now have achieved the reputation they merit. As a matter of fact, a number of Pomerol vineyards consistently sell their wines for more than the second growths of the Médoc.

The vineyards of Pomerol are fairly small, and its most famous property, Château Pétrus, only produces about three thousand cases a year (compared to twenty thousand to thirty thousand cases produced by many Médoc châteaux). The comparatively small sizes of the Pomerol and Saint-Emilion vineyards probably accounts for their late-flowering reputations both in France and abroad. Vineyards were originally established in these two districts by a middle class looking for "a small property in the country." In contrast, the great vineyards of the Médoc were established in the early eighteenth century by an aristocratic class that was able to carve out much bigger estates in that undeveloped area. The greater production of the Médoc châteaux and the higher social standing of its owners gave this district a momentum from the very beginning. The Classification of 1855 did not even consider the vineyards of Saint-Emilion and Pomerol, and to this day, their small size has made them less well-known.

There is very little regional Pomerol available, as its wines are mostly sold under the names of individual châteaux. Pomerols have a distinctive full-flavored and earthy quality and they generally mature more quickly than do the wines of Saint-Emilion. No classification has ever been established for Pomerol, but the following list indicates the best, and best known, of its vineyards. Château Pétrus stands apart, on a level with the first growths of the Médoc.

POMEROL

Château Pétrus

Château Beauregard	Château Latour-Pomerol
Château Certan-de-May	Clos l'Eglise
Château Certan-Giraud	Domaine de l'Eglise
Château Clinet	Château l'Eglise-Clinet
Château Gazin	Château l'Evangile
Château La Conseillante	Château Nénin
Château Lafleur	Château Petit-Village
Château Lafleur-Pétrus	Château Rouget
Château Lagrange	Château Trotanoy
Château La Pointe	Vieux-Château Certan

Other Pomerol properties include:

Château de Sales
Château Taillefer
Clos René

Sauternes

The luscious, sweet dessert wines of Sauternes are among the most unusual in the world, and they are produced by a unique and expensive process that can take place only in certain years. The Sauternes district is geographically contained within the southern part of Graves, about thirty miles from Bordeaux. Wines produced in the inner district of Barsac are, technically speaking, Sauternes as well, but these wines are entitled to be marketed under their own *appellation contrôlée* of Barsac. Some vineyards use the *appellation contrôlée* Barsac, others use Sauternes, and some use both names to make the most of the situation.

Sauternes is always a sweet wine. The name is used (often without the final *s*) to label wines from other countries that range in taste from mellow to dry. There is certainly no such thing as a dry Sauternes from Bordeaux. The wine is made by leaving the grapes (Sémillon and Sauvignon Blanc, plus a little Muscadelle) on the vine beyond the normal harvest time. A combination of moisture (light rains or dew) and continued sunny days will result in the appearance of a white mold, *botrytis cinerea,* on the grapes themselves. This *pourriture noble,* or noble rot, shrivels up the grapes in such a way that the resulting juice is extremely rich in sugar. Trained workers must return to the vineyards several times, picking out the bunches that have been affected by this beneficial mold. When the grapes are pressed, the juice ferments to produce extraordinarily luscious wines that contain sizable amounts of residual sugar. Sauternes is, of course, a completely natural table wine, not fortified as are Port and Sherry.

The proper combination of climatic conditions necessary to produce Sauternes does not happen very often. Furthermore, the yield per acre from these shriveled grapes is considerably lower than for dry wines. Nevertheless, Sauternes is not an expensive wine, and good vintages of the best châteaux are available for three to four dollars and are not much more expensive than the regional blends marketed by the various Bordeaux shippers. The reason for this is that Sauternes is no longer as popular as it once was, and is therefore a tremendous value for those who

enjoy its distinctive taste. At one time it was appropriate
to serve a Sauternes with a first course of fish, and this
practice still exists today in Bordeaux to a limited extent.
Sauternes is best served with dessert or to accompany ripe
fruit, such as peaches or melon. The wine is not to everyone's taste, and you should be careful about serving it at a
dinner with a number of guests. But you must not deny
yourself the experience of tasting a bottle of this unique
wine, preferably as produced by one of the best châteaux.

Some shippers market both a Sauternes and a Haut-
Sauternes. There is no legal difference between them, nor
does one come from a better part of the district. Each
shipper will probably make his Haut-Sauternes a bit
sweeter, but that is entirely up to him.

There is one vineyard in Sauternes that is considerably
more famous than all of the others, and that is Château
d'Yquem. Its wines sell for ten dollars or more a bottle
in good vintages, and its 250 acres constitute one of the
most famous vineyards in the world.

The wines of Sauternes were classified in 1855 along with
those of the Médoc and a great many of these château-
bottled wines are imported into this country.

THE CLASSIFICATION OF 1855
FOR SAUTERNES AND BARSAC

Grand Premier Crû—First Great Growth
Château d'Yquem

Premiers Crûs—First Growths

Château La Tour-Blanche	Château Climens
Clos Haut-Peyraguey	Château Guiraud
Château Lafaurie-Peyraguey	Château Rieussec
Château de Rayne-Vigneau	Château Rabaud-Promis
Château de Suduiraut	Château Sigalas-Rabaud
Château Coutet	

Deuxièmes Crûs—Second Growths

Château Myrat	Château D'Arche
Château Doisy-Daëne	Château Filhot
Château Doisy-Védrines	Château Broustet

Château Nairac
Château Caillou
Château Suau

Château de Malle
Château Romer
Château Lamothe

BURGUNDY

Burgundy is perhaps the most evocative of all wine names and conveys different impressions to different people. The historian knows Burgundy as an independent duchy that was annexed to France in the late fifteenth century. The decorator associates the name with a deep red color, although Burgundy produces white wines that are among the finest in the world. Many consumers think of Burgundy as a full-flavored red wine that can come from any one of several countries, although the province of Burgundy is strictly delimited and lies in east-central France, about one hundred miles from the Swiss border. And to many wine drinkers Burgundy means wines that are rich and heavy, although many of the finest Burgundies are noted for their delicacy, finesse, and refinement.

All of Burgundy produces about one-third as much wine as Bordeaux, but 80 percent of this is from Beaujolais and the Mâconnais. Perhaps a more relevant comparison would be between the main districts of Bordeaux, which are the Médoc, Saint-Emilion, Pomerol, and Graves, and the heart of Burgundy—the Côte d'Or—which produces such famous red and white wines as Chambertin, Pommard, Beaune, and Montrachet. There is only one-fourth as much of this top Burgundy as there is of the best of Bordeaux, which is another way of saying that good Burgundy will always be scarce and expensive. The combination of a few poor vintages and some good recent vintages with smaller than average crops have now made the wines of the Côte d'Or more expensive than ever, and on the average the most expensive wines of any region in the world.

The vineyards of Burgundy are spread out and are divided into several main districts: Chablis, to the north; the Côte d'Or, which consists of the Côte de Nuits and the Côte de Beaune; and to the south, the Chalonnais, the

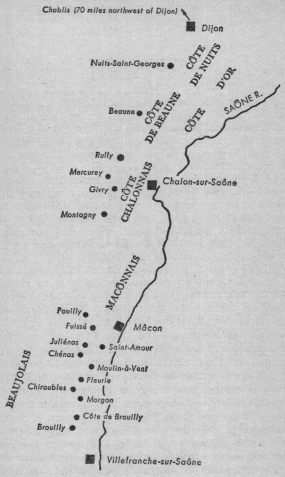

Chablis (70 miles northwest of Dijon)

Dijon

CÔTE DE NUITS

D'OR

Nuits-Saint-Georges

CÔTE DE BEAUNE

CÔTE

SAÔNE R.

Beaune

Rully

Mercurey

CÔTE CHALONNAIS

Chalon-sur-Saône

Givry

Montagny

MÂCONNAIS

Pouilly

Fuissé

Mâcon

Juliénas

Saint-Amour

Chénas

BEAUJOLAIS

Moulin-à-Vent

Fleurie

Chiroubles

Morgon

Côte de Brouilly

Brouilly

Villefranche-sur-Saône

The Burgundy Districts

Mâconnais (including Pouilly-Fuissé), and the vast Beaujolais district.

White Burgundy from any district must be made entirely from the Chardonnay grape, although there is a small amount of Pinot Blanc still planted in a few scattered vineyards. (It is now believed that the famous white wine grape of Burgundy—traditionally called the Pinot Chardonnay—is not actually a member of the Pinot family.) Red Burgundy from the Côte d'Or is made entirely from the Pinot Noir; the Gamay is used in Beaujolais and the Mâconnais. There is a substantial amount of white wine—rarely marketed in this country—made from the lesser Aligoté grape, and entitled only to the appellation Bourgogne Aligoté. Red wines that are made from a mixture of Pinot Noir and Gamay in the Côte d'Or are labeled Bourgogne-Passe-Tous-Grains.

Chablis

Almost a hundred miles north of the Côte d'Or, just off the road to Paris, is the town of Chablis, whose vineyards are properly considered a part of Burgundy. Although Chablis may be the most famous of all white wine names, the number of consumers who have actually drunk wine produced from vineyards around the town itself can not be many. The name Chablis is used so frequently to describe white wines from other countries that it is well to remember that true Chablis comes from certain chalky hillsides planted in the Chardonnay grape, and subject to the particular climatic conditions of these northerly vineyards. The result is a bone-dry, crisp wine with a comparatively big-bodied flavor and a refreshing touch of acidity. Years with too much sunshine do not produce typical Chablis, and such wines tend to be a bit heavy and flabby in character.

Chablis itself is very much a wine village, and along its streets little signs hang out at frequent intervals, indicating that wine can be tasted and bought from the vineyard proprietor who lives inside. Most growers own vines in several places, and consequently make Chablis of different appellations. The lowest appellation is *Petit Chablis*, from land farthest from the town itself. The wine is very enjoyable when drunk young, but will not keep its qualities for more than two or three years. *Chablis* is the basic village appellation. There are then two dozen specified vineyards whose wines are entitled to be called *premier crû*, with or without the vineyard name indicated. It happens that there is as much *premier crû* Chablis produced as there is plain Chablis, and these two appellations account for about 80 percent of the total. The top 5 percent comes from seven vineyards of *grand crû* status, and these wines will generally have more depth of character and style to them.

At one time production of Chablis was fairly erratic, as the vineyards were subject to sudden frosts, which often destroyed most of the crop. In recent years the growers have been making the most of modern agricultural equipment to heat the vineyards when the temperature drops too low. They have also been producing more wine than ever from the same area. Inescapably, quality suffers and some of the wines available, even from individual growers, lack the flavor that one looks for in these unique wines.

Chablis Grand Crû

Blanchots	Les Preuses
Bougros	Valmur
Les Clos	Vaudésir
Grenouilles	

Chablis Premier Crû

There are nearly two dozen classified vineyards, of which these are most frequently seen on labels:

Beugnon	Montée de Tonnerre
Fourchaume	Séchet
Les Fôrets	Vaillon
Mont de Milieu	Vaulorent

The Côte d'Or

The Côte d'Or, or Golden Slope, gets its name from the appearance of these hillside vineyards when they have taken on their autumn foliage. The vineyards of the Côte d'Or begin just below Dijon and continue, with a break midway, for about thirty miles down to Santenay. This

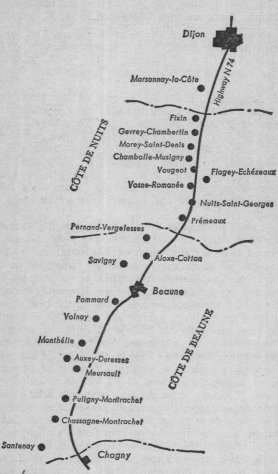

Dijon

Marsannay-la-Côte

Highway N 74

Fixin

Gevrey-Chambertin

Morey-Saint-Denis

Chambolle-Musigny

Vougeot

Flagey-Echézeaux

Vosne-Romanée

CÔTE DE NUITS

Nuits-Saint-Georges

Pernand-Vergelesses

Prémeaux

Savigny

Aloxe-Corton

Beaune

Pommard

Volnay

CÔTE DE BEAUNE

Monthélie

Auxey-Duresses

Meursault

Puligny-Montrachet

Chassagne-Montrachet

Santenay

Chagny

The Côte d'Or: The Côte de Nuits and the Côte de Beaune

strip of soil, never more than half a mile wide, produces only 15 percent of all the Burgundies made, but it is here that are situated the famous villages and vineyards, which most people associate with the name Burgundy. The northern half is the Côte de Nuits, and known primarily for its red wines. The Côte de Beaune, to the south, produces more red wine than white but is more famous for its superb white wines.

Red Burgundies, about 85 percent of the Côte d'Or wines, are considered easier to enjoy than Bordeaux, as they are softer, fuller, rounder wines. They have a more beguiling bouquet, generally described as more perfumed, and they seem to taste less austerely dry than claret. Unfortunately, many consumers imagine that Burgundies are heavy, almost sweet wines, as a result of the inferior blends that have been marketed for so long: such wines have nothing of the elegance and balance of the best wines of Burgundy.

While good Burgundies may be very appealing to many wine drinkers, they are also considerably more difficult to understand than are the wines of Bordeaux. In the first place, there are more village names to remember in the Côte d'Or than in Bordeaux: fourteen or so that are important, and several others that are less frequently encountered, and that therefore provide some of the best values. Apart from these village names, and two or three district names, there are thirty-one individual vineyards, officially rated as *grands crûs,* which are legally entitled to their own *appellation contrôlée.* That is, the name of the vineyard appears by itself on a label (Chambertin, Montrachet, Musigny) without the name of its village of origin. In Bordeaux, of course, even the best vineyards bear a commune or district appellation, which makes it considerably easier to place them geographically. Thus, Château Lafite-Rothschild has the *appellation contrôlée* Pauillac on its label, and Château Haut-Brion is identified as a Graves.

Not only is it necessary for the intelligent buyer of good Burgundy to know his wine villages and to have some familiarity with the *grands crûs,* but one other important factor further complicates his choice of wine. Almost all of the vineyards in Burgundy, which are fairly small to begin with, are owned by several different growers. For example, Montrachet is 19 acres in size, and has over a dozen owners. The 23 acres of Grands-Echézeaux are divided among ten owners; and Clos de Vougeot, whose 125 acres make it the biggest vineyard in Burgundy, has more than eighty owners today. This multiple ownership can be traced back to the French Revolution, when large domains owned by the church and by members of the nobility were confiscated and sold in small parcels to the local farmers. The laws of inheritance in Burgundy have made these holdings even smaller, whereas in Bordeaux the large châteaux are maintained as corporate entities and have continued intact. Evidently each grower will decide for himself when to replant old vines, how far back to prune, when to harvest, and exactly how to vinify his wines. The result is a number of different wines of different quality from the same vineyard. Two people can discuss the merits of Château Latour 1959, which they enjoyed separately, and be certain they are talking about the same wine. Two people comparing notes on a previously consumed bottle of Chambertin 1962 or Volnay Caillerets 1955 must first establish whose wine each was drinking.

Not every grower markets his wines with his own name. Most of the wines are sold in barrel to the big shipping firms in Burgundy, who blend together wines from each appellation to make what they hope will be a consistently dependable Beaune, Pommard, or Nuits-Saint-Georges. The demand for the best-known wines of Burgundy has unfortunately led to "stretching" them with lesser wines from other regions. To protect themselves and to obtain a justifiably higher price for their wines, a number of growers have taken to bottling their wines themselves, as do the châteaux of Bordeaux. Such wines bear the words *Mis en bouteilles au domaine, Mis au domaine,* or *Mis en bouteilles à la propriété,* and these estate-bottled wines are the Burgundian equivalent of the château-bottled wines of Bordeaux. Words such as *mis en bouteilles dans nos caves,* or bottled in our cellars, are meaningless, as are the English words *estate bottled* without the French equivalent.

There are three important levels of quality in the Côte d'Or: village wines, *premiers crûs,* and *grands crûs.* This rating system is incorporated into the official *appellation contrôlée* laws for Burgundy and was based on historical precedent and careful analysis of each vineyard. There has never been an official classification of the Côte d'Or vineyards similar in status to the 1855 classification for the Médoc, but an attempt was made in 1861. Each of the best vineyards was named a *Tête de Cuvée,* and this traditional distinction is still found on some labels, particularly for those vineyards that did not merit *grand crû* status under the *appellation contrôlée* laws. One indication of how difficult it must have been to rate each one of the small Burgundian vineyards is the fact that they are traditionally referred to as *climats.* In other words, it is understood that rain, for example, will affect each plot of land in a certain way, depending on the ability of the subsoil to absorb water, that its position on a slope will determine its exposure to the sun, and so forth. Perhaps a modern way of translating *climat* would be micro-climate.

The principal wine villages are shown on the map, and will be discussed in detail. One confusing aspect of some of these village names came about in the late nineteenth century when a number of villages appended to their names that of their most famous individual vineyard. Thus Gevrey became Gevrey-Chambertin, Chambolle became Chambolle-Musigny, Nuits changed to Nuits-Saint-Georges, and so on. As the great vineyard of Montrachet is partly situated in both Chassagne and Puligny, both of these villages added its name to their own. Consumers will sometimes imagine that they have drunk the specific product of a great vineyard when in fact they have been served a village wine, which can come from vines anywhere in the named village. It must be pointed out, however, that these villages do not produce a great deal of wine and their names on a label should by no means be thought of as a regional appellation. For example, Saint-Emilion produces twenty times as much wine as does Pommard, and the Médoc village of Saint-Estèphe makes four times more wine than does the village of Nuits-Saint-Georges.

The *premier crû* vineyards of the Côte d'Or are not difficult to spot because their names follow those of their respective villages. Thus, some *premier crû* wines from Volnay are Volnay Caillerets, Volnay Champans, Volnay Clos des Ducs, and so forth. Other *premier crû* wines from different villages include Gevrey-Chambertin, Clos Saint-

Jacques; Pommard, Les Rugiens; Chassagne-Montrachet, Clos de Boudriottes; and so on. Not infrequently you will see the words *premier crû* after a village name, without the name of a specific vineyard, such as Chassagne-Montrachet *Premier Crû.* This simply indicates that the wine comes from more than one *premier crû* vineyard, or that the producer felt that these words would make his wine more saleable than the name of a specific, but unfamiliar, vineyard.

The highest rating in the Côte d'Or is that of *grand crû,* and the thirty-one wines so classed are listed, vineyard by vineyard, along with some of the better-known *premiers crûs.* If you recognize the village names, certain *grand crû* vineyards are easy to locate: Chambertin, Musigny, Montrachet, Romanée-Saint-Vivant, for example. Other *grand crû* names, however, bear no relation to that of their village of origin, and only homework will lead to familiarity: for example, Clos de la Roche, Richebourg, Bonnes Mares. *Grand crû* wines account for perhaps 5 percent of all the wines of the Côte de Nuits and Côte de Beaune, and they are always expensive. They are also among the greatest red and white wines in the world, and their study will be repaid by their excellence.

A grower in Burgundy does not produce a single wine, as does a Bordeaux châteaux. He deliberately has vines in several vineyards, and often in two or three adjoining villages, so that he is protected to some extent from the hailstorms and frosts that occasionally occur, and which often affect only a very small area at a time. Of course, another factor leading to scattered holdings is that domains in Burgundy are built up slowly as money is accumulated and vines become available for sale.

A visitor to a Bordeaux château will be taken on a tour of the *chai,* see hundreds of barrels of new wine aging in spacious surroundings, and then be offered a glass of one, or perhaps two, vintages currently in wood. Visiting a cellar in Burgundy means crowding in among barrels piled two or three high, and a tasting will include as many as a dozen different wines from different villages and vineyards. A famous Bordeaux château may produce fifteen thousand to thirty thousand cases of a single wine in a year. A Burgundian grower whose domain is big enough to justify estate bottling may produce only five hundred to one thousand cases, made up of several wines. His share of a *grand crû* vineyard may only be big enough to produce one barrel, or twenty-five cases, a year.

It becomes evident, then, that whereas in Bordeaux a knowledge of the main districts and of a few major châteaux will get you off to a good start, knowing Burgundy is a bit more time-consuming. You must know the villages, a few *grand crû* vineyards, and then pay strict attention to the shipper or grower whose wine you are drinking. There are a few serious shippers in Burgundy whose wines are consistently well made and can be consumed with pleasure. If there is a fault that can be leveled against them, however, it is that the wines of any individual shipper tend to have a family resemblance that cuts across the various appellations. The reason is simple enough: each shipper has some ideas about what a good Burgundy should taste like and tries to maintain his standards, sometimes at the expense of the individual characteristics of a village or vineyard. For that reason, many consumers search out the best of the estate-bottled wines, and a number of individual growers have now become well-known in this country. Many fine estate-bottled Burgundies are shipped by the Alexis Lichine Company, and those selected by Frank Schoonmaker are also noteworthy. Among the best of the Burgundy shippers are the firms of Joseph Drouhin, Louis Latour, and Louis Jadot.

What follows is a closer look at the individual wine villages of the Côte d'Or, starting with the Côte de Nuits. With a few exceptions, which will be noted, all the wines of the Côte de Nuits are red.

Just below Dijon is the little village of Marsannay whose wines have begun to be seen over here, especially the delightful Rosé de Marsannay (from the Pinot Noir grape) and the Pinot Noir de Marsannay.

Fixin, pronounced by its inhabitants as *fee-san,* produces less than a tenth as much wine as Nuits-Saint-Georges or Pommard, but good wines from its best vineyards can occasionally be found here.

The next village is world famous: Gevrey-Chambertin.

Its two principal vineyards, Chambertin and Chambertin-Clos de Bèze, sit side by side and extend for about seventy acres. Vines were planted around the abbey of Clos de Bèze as early as the seventh century, and its wines soon achieved a high reputation. In the thirteenth century, the story goes, a farmer named Bertin planted vines in the adjacent field, which was known as *champ de Bertin,* or Bertin's field. Although these two vineyards are now known for their outstanding red wines, it's interesting to note that at one time there was also a white Chambertin, an early example of trial and error. Most of the proprietors of one vineyard own vines in the other, so it's hard to distinguish between the two plots. Moreover, while Chambertin can only be sold as such, wines from Chambertin-Clos de Bèze can also be sold simply as Chambertin.

There are, in addition to these two vineyards, seven other vineyards of *grand crû* stature bearing the name Chambertin, including Chapelle-Chambertin, Charmes-Chambertin, Latricières-Chambertin, Ruchottes-Chambertin, Mazys-Chambertin, Mazoyères-Chambertin, and Griotte-Chambertin. The two great vineyards produce about ten thousand cases a year, the other seven together about twenty thousand cases. The best wines of this village are the biggest-bodied of all Burgundies and at their best are unequaled.

The village of Morey-Saint-Denis lies between the considerably more famous ones of Gevrey-Chambertin and Chambolle-Musigny. Its name is not often seen on wine labels here partly because many of its growers, who own vines in the adjoining towns, market their wines under the name of those better-known villages; and also because one-third of the wine produced in Morey is of *grand crû* class and is sold without reference to the village. These vineyards are Clos de la Roche, Clos Saint-Denis, Clos de Tart, and a small part of Bonnes Mares. The first is by far the biggest, and Clos de Tart is one of the few vineyards in Burgundy under single ownership.

Chambolle-Musigny is known for its elegant and distinguished wines, and its two *grand crû* vineyards, Musigny and most of Bonnes Mares, are in the top rank of all Burgundies. A very small amount of white wine, Musigny Blanc, is also produced in that vineyard.

The little hamlet of Vougeot produces some attractive

red wines sold as such, but its fame is derived from its single great vineyard, Clos de Vougeot. First planted in vines by the Cistercian monks in the twelfth century, its 125 acres have been maintained as a single vineyard throughout the centuries. The vineyard is so extensive, however, that some parcels are much better situated than others. Moreover, there are so many proprietors who own vines in this vineyard—some of them producing only one or two barrels a year—that quality varies considerably from bottle to bottle. The Clos de Vougeot itself is now the headquarters of the Chevaliers du Tastevin, an organization founded to promote the wines of Burgundy, and the large hall is frequently the scene of convivial dinners. An excellent white wine from Vougeot, Clos Blanc de Vougeot, is often seen in this country.

Flagey-Echézeaux does not have its own village appellation, but it does contain two vineyards of *grand cru* status. Grands-Echézeaux, which adjoins Clos de Vougeot, is divided among several proprietors. The vineyard name Echézeaux can in fact be used by any one of ten vineyards whose wines can also be marketed as Vosne-Romanée. Its production is three times that of Grands-Echézeaux.

Vosne-Romanée produces village wines of a fairly high level, and its best vineyards are among the most famous and most expensive in the world. The village includes the four-acre vineyard of Romanée-Conti, whose wines sell for twenty to forty dollars a bottle. The property is owned by the Domaine de la Romanée-Conti, which also owns all of La Tâche and parts of Richebourg, Grands-Echézeaux, Echézeaux, and Montrachet. The Domaine is also making and marketing the wine from that part of the Romanée-Saint-Vivant vineyard owned by the widow of General Marey-Monge. Another vineyard, which does not have official *grand cru* status but which is on a par with the best of Burgundy, is La Grande Rue. Its three acres are situated between Romanée-Conti and La Tâche, and it is owned entirely by Henri Lamarche. Although the *grand cru* wines of Vosne-Romanée are all expensive and will become even more so, a number of *premiers crus* produce excellent wines as well.

Nuits-Saint-Georges is the biggest village in the Côte de Nuits, and its wines are among the best known of all Bur-

gundies. Nuits-Saint-Georges and Gevrey-Chambertin produce between them about half the village wines of the Côte
de Nuits, but even this is not enough to satisfy the world
demand, and quality varies from label to label. The appellation Côte de Nuits-Villages is a regional one for the whole
district, and such wines invariably come from the less important towns of the Côte de Nuits, such as Corgoloin,
Comblanchien, and Brochon, not from Nuits-Saint-Georges
itself. The wines of Prémeaux, which adjoins Nuits-Saint-
Georges, can be marketed as Nuits-Saint-Georges.

At this point, the Golden Slope disappears for a few
miles and, when it reappears, it becomes the Côte de
Beaune. The first important village is Aloxe-Corton, dominated by the impressive hill of Corton, on whose slopes lie
the best vineyards. Aloxe-Corton (locally pronounced *ah-
loss*) makes some very agreeable red wines, but the best of
its wines are labeled Corton, often with a supplementary
plot name. In other words, Aloxe-Corton is a village appellation, and its *grand crû,* logically enough, is Corton, but
there are several other vineyards on the hill of Corton, such
as Corton Clos du Roi, Corton Bressandes, and Corton
Maréchaudes, whose wines will often surpass those labeled
simply Corton.

Until now, all of the wines discussed have been red, but
in Aloxe-Corton we encounter the first of the important
white wine vineyards, Corton-Charlemagne. In the Côte de
Beaune the only *grand crû* vineyard producing red wines is
Corton; all the others produce white wines. Corton-Charlemagne bears testimony to the influence of the Emperor
Charlemagne, who owned vineyards in Burgundy in the
eighth century. At its best, it is a superlative wine of great
power and breed. The vineyard actually produces more
wine than any other *grand crû* except Clos de Vougeot and
Corton: its principal owner is the firm of Louis Latour.

Pernand-Vergelesses lies behind Aloxe-Corton, and adjoins it: most of its wines are sold as Aloxe-Corton. Sa-
vigny-les-Beaune is one of the biggest wine-producing
villages of the entire slope, and almost all of its wines are
red. Being less well-known, this excellent wine is less expensive than those of its more illustrious neighbors.

Beaune is not only the center of the Côte de Beaune, but
of Burgundy itself. It is the biggest town of all, and most of

the shippers are headquartered here. Every year, on the third Sunday in November, the town is host to buyers from all over the world who arrive to take part in the wine auction at the Hospices de Beaune and in the general festivity that prevails for three days.

The Hospices de Beaune is a charitable hospital built in the fifteenth century by Nicolas Rollin and his wife Guigone de Salins. Over the years vineyard parcels have been bequeathed to the Hospices, and the money obtained from the sale by auction of their wine is used to support the institution. The wines are generally considered to be a bit overpriced, but the prices they fetch have a great deal to do with determining the general price levels of the year's crop throughout the Côte d'Or.

The Hospices de Beaune now owns about 125 acres in several villages, and produces fifteen thousand or more cases a year. The wines are auctioned in lots identified for the most part by the name of the donor rather than that of an individual vineyard. One cannot simply refer to a bottle of Hospices de Beaune wine, but must properly identify it with the village and the specific parcel, or *cuvée,* among the thirty-odd that make up the Hospices's holdings. Among the most famous are Beaune—*Cuvée* Nicolas Rollin; Beaune—*Cuvée* Guigone de Salins; Corton—*Cuvée* Docteur Peste; Pommard—*Cuvée* Dames de la Charité. The Hospices's white wines are almost all from Meursault and include Meursault-Charmes—*Cuvée* Albert Grivault and Meursault Genevrières—*Cuvée* Baudot.

Beaune produces a great deal of wine by Burgundian standards and 95 percent of it is red. A wine labeled Côte de Beaune-Villages, often a good value, comes not from Beaune, but from villages of lesser standing whose wines are seldom marketed under their own unimpressive names.

Pommard is probably the most famous name in Burgundy and there can be no doubt, unfortunately, that some of the red wine sold as Pommard doesn't even bear a nodding acquaintance with the village itself. If you want to drink a good Pommard, with the particular *terroir,* or undertaste, that characterizes these wines, your best bet is to look for an individual vineyard wine that is estate bottled. Although there are no *grands crûs* in Pommard, most experts consider that the *têtes de cuvées* of the 1861 classification, Rugiens and Epenots, deserve the same status today.

Volnay, despite its simple name, has not achieved the same popularity in the U. S. as Pommard and Nuits-Saint-Georges. Its elegant red wines, at best, display a delicacy and finesse that belie the popular misconception of Burgundy as a heavy wine.

Meursault is the first of the white wine villages. Its vineyards, along with those of Chassagne-Montrachet and Puligny-Montrachet, produce almost all of the greatest white wines of Burgundy and of the world. Meursault actually produces more wine than the other two villages combined, and its wines are characterized by a certain tangy dryness that sets them apart from the others. Although there are no *grand crû* vineyards in this village, Perrières and Genevrières are considered its best sites. Some red wine is produced in Meursault, notably Meursault-Blagny. Part of the Santenots vineyard is also planted in Pinot Noir: the whites are sold as Meursault-Santenots, the reds as Volnay-Santenots.

Set back from the main highway are the two villages of Monthélie and Auxey-Duresses. Monthélie produces red wines with the lightness of its neighbor, Volnay. Auxey-Duresses makes both reds and whites, and both are very agreeable. Wines from less commercialized villages such as these are worth looking for.

Chassagne-Montrachet is famous for its white wines, but in fact two-thirds of its production is red, and these agreeable wines are still relatively inexpensive. The white wines of Chassagne are, of course, outstanding, and within the village are parts of two great vineyards, Montrachet and Bâtard-Montrachet, as well as all four acres of Criots-Bâtard-Montrachet.

Puligny-Montrachet makes white wines only and of a very high quality. The rest of Montrachet and Bâtard-Montrachet are situated within its borders, as well as all of Chevalier-Montrachet and Bienvenue-Bâtard-Montrachet.

Montrachet is considered to be the best vineyard in the world for dry white wines, and it can indeed produce superlative wines. It's also true that not all of its several owners are equally careful, and when you spend ten to fifteen dollars for a bottle you are likely to be paying as much for its fame and scarcity as for the quality of the wine. The other *grand crû* vineyards should not be scorned, nor should the very excellent village and *premier crû* wines from good sources.

Santenay is the last village of note in the Côte de Beaune, and its agreeable wines, almost all red, are well worth trying.

CÔTE DE NUITS: *Red Wines*

Village	Grands Crûs	Premiers Crûs
Fixin		Clos de la Perrière
		Clos du Chapitre
		Les Hervelets
		Les Arvelets
Gevrey-Chambertin	Chambertin	Clos Saint-Jacques
	Chambertin-Clos de Bèze	Varoilles
	Latricières-Chambertin	Les Cazetiers
	Mazys-Chambertin	Combe-au-Moine
	Mazoyères-Chambertin	
	Ruchottes-Chambertin	
	Chapelle-Chambertin	
	Charmes-Chambertin	
	Griotte-Chambertin	
Morey-Saint Denis	Clos de Tart	Clos des Lambrays
	Clos Saint-Denis	Clos Bussière
	Clos de la Roche	
	Bonnes Mares (part)	
Chambolle-Musigny	Musigny	Les Amoureuses
	Bonnes Mares (part)	Les Charmes
Vougeot	Clos de Vougeot	
Flagey-Echézeaux	Grands-Echézeaux	
	Echézeaux	
Vosne-Romanée	Romanée-Conti	La Grande Rue
	La Romanée	Les Gaudichots
	La Tâche	Les Beaumonts
	Richebourg	Les Malconsorts
	Romanée-Saint-Vivant	Les Suchots
		Aux Brûlées
		Clos des Réas

Village	Grands Crûs	Premiers Crûs
Nuits-Saint-Georges (including Prémeaux)		Les Saint-Georges
		Les Vaucrains
		Les Cailles
		Les Pruliers
		Les Porrets
		Aux Boudots
		La Richemone
		Clos de la Maréchale
		Clos des Corvées
		Aux Perdrix
		Les Didiers
		Aux Thorey

The Côte de Nuits produces very little white wine, but the following can be found here: Musigny Blanc, Clos Blanc de Vougeot, and Nuits-Saint-Georges Les Perrières.

CÔTE DE BEAUNE: *Red Wines*

Village	Grands Crûs	Premiers Crûs
Pernand-Vergelesses		Ile-des-Vergelesses
Aloxe-Corton	Le Corton	Corton Clos du Roi
		Corton Bressandes
		Corton Maréchaudes
		Corton Renardes
		Corton Les Meix
Savigny-les-Beaune		Les Vergelesses
		Les Marconnets
		La Dominode
		Les Jarrons
		Les Lavières
Beaune		Les Grèves
		Les Fèves
		Les Marconnets
		Les Bressandes
		Les Clos des Mouches
		Les Cent Vignes
		Clos du Roi
		Les Avaux
Pommard		Les Epenots
		Les Rugiens
		Le Clos Blanc
		La Platière
		Les Pézerolles
		Les Chaponnières

Village	Grands Crûs	Premiers Crûs
Volnay		Clos des Ducs
		Les Caillerets
		Les Champans
		Les Fremiets
		Santenots
		Le Clos des Chênes
Monthélie		Les Champs Fuillots
Auxey-Duresses		Les Duresses
		Clos du Val
Chassagne-Montrachet		Clos Saint-Jean
		Clos de la Boudriotte
		Morgeot
		La Maltroie
		Les Caillerets
Santenay		Gravières
		Clos Tavannes

CÔTE DE BEAUNE: *White Wines*

Village	Grands Crûs	Premiers Crûs
Aloxe-Corton	Corton Charlemagne	
	Charlemagne	
Beaune		Les Clos des Mouches
Meursault		Les Perrières
		Les Genevrières
		La Goutte d'Or
		Charmes
		Santenots
		Blagny
		Poruzot
Puligny-Montrachet	Montrachet (part)	Les Combettes
	Bâtard-Montrachet (part)	Le Champ Canet
		Les Caillerets
	Chevalier-Montrachet	Les Pucelles
	Bienvenue-Bâtard-Montrachet	Les Chalumeaux
		Les Folatières
		Clavoillon
		Les Referts
Chassagne-Montrachet	Montrachet (part)	Les Ruchottes
	Bâtard-Montrachet (part)	Morgeot
		Les Caillerets
	Criots-Bâtard-Montrachet	Les Chenevottes

Southern Burgundy

Southern Burgundy is made up of three districts, the Chalonnais, the Mâconnais, and Beaujolais. Beaujolais is well-known for its red wines, and the Mâconnais contains the inner appellation of Pouilly-Fuissé, but the Chalonnais wines are not established in world markets, despite their resemblance and proximity to the famous wines of Burgundy. The two most interesting villages in the Chalonnais, which takes its name from the city of Chalon-sur-Saône, are Givry and Mercurey, noted primarily for their red wines. Made from the Pinot Noir, and governed by *appellation contrôlée* laws very similar to those in effect in the Côte d'Or, the wines are, not surprisingly, quite similar to those of the Côte de Beaune, although a bit lighter in body. The best examples are good, well balanced, and generally more attractive than many of the expensive wines from better-known villages. Givry produces very little wine, but Mercurey makes about as much red wine as does Gevrey-Chambertin or Pommard.

The Mâcon district produces red and white wine as well as some rosé, and the wines have long been available here. For the most part they are neither expensive nor remarkable. The red, made from the Gamay, lacks the style of the best wines of Beaujolais. The whites, from the Chardonnay, are generally better wines. In recent years some shippers have been marketing the white wines of Mâcon by their traditional varietal name—Pinot Chardonnay—in imitation of the approach used by the better California wineries. Because French law requires that Mâcon Blanc must be made entirely from the named grape and because there is so much of this wine available for sale, a Pinot Chardonnay from Burgundy is often a better value than all but the very best examples from California.

The most famous wine of the Mâconnais is Pouilly-Fuissé. The appellation is limited to wines coming from the four hamlets of Solutré-Pouilly, Fuissé, Chaintré, and Vergisson. Although this wine is extremely popular and is ubiquitous on all restaurant wine lists, there is actually not much of it made. An abundant year will produce only 250,000 cases and recent vintages have produced considerably less. As a result of increased demand and short crops, there has been a rapid rise in the price of this wine at the vineyard, and it is now at nearly the levels of the village wines of Meursault, Chassagne, and Puligny.

Close to the four communes of Pouilly-Fuissé are those of Loché and Vinzelles. They produce about one-tenth as much wine, which is marketed as Pouilly-Loché and Pouilly-Vinzelles. The wines are, of course, very similar to those of Pouilly-Fuissé, although slightly less elegant and less full. They are also less expensive.

BEAUJOLAIS

Beaujolais is one of the best known of all red wines, and in this country it certainly outsells those from any other French district. Many people think that Beaujolais is Beaujolais and are willing to settle for an inexpensive example when they want a cheap red wine. Compared to the best wines of Bordeaux and the Côte d'Or, those of Beaujolais are not as exciting, as scarce, or as difficult to understand, but there is actually quite a variation in price, quality, and taste available from this vast wine district in southern Burgundy. With the wines of the Côte de Nuits and Côte de Beaune becoming increasingly expensive, it is worth taking a close look at the variety of Beaujolais, as this includes some of the most enjoyable wines produced anywhere, and consequently some of the best values. What's more, there are many occasions when an excellent Beaujolais would be not only more appropriate but also more enjoyable than an old bottle of Lafite-Rothschild, which requires a certain amount of attention, care, and time to enjoy.

The Beaujolais district begins near Mâcon (about sixty miles south of Beaune) and stretches down to the outskirts of Lyons, forty-five miles farther south. The vineyard district stretches about ten miles across, along the western bank of the Saône River. The region takes its name from the village of Beaujeu, originally a barony established more than a thousand years ago. Beaujeu is no longer an important town, and the center of the Beaujolais wine trade now is Villefranche, which lies about halfway between Mâcon and Lyon. The hills and valleys of Beaujolais are probably the most picturesque and agreeable vineyard district in France, and the landscape has charmed many tourists who have come to the area in search of Roman ruins and to visit the remains of the monastery of Cluny with its gigantic twelfth-century church.

In an abundant vintage, the Beaujolais district produces about six or seven million cases of wine, although a great deal of this is never actually bottled, being served directly from the barrel in the restaurants of Lyons and Paris. (Small amounts of agreeable white and rosé are also produced, but more than 99 percent of Beaujolais is red.) Beaujolais is made from the Gamay grape. Although this variety is scorned in the vineyards of the Côte d'Or, the Gamay comes into its own in the granitic soil of southern Burgundy and produces wines much more charming and agreeable than would be produced from the Pinot Noir. The wines of Beaujolais are at their best when consumed young, before they are three years old, and the wines are vinified with this in mind. Vatting is limited to three days or less so that a minimum of tannin is imparted to the wine. The wines are then bottled—and often consumed—within six months of the vintage, so that they maintain the freshness and fruit that make Beaujolais so agreeable.

Many Paris restaurants feature a *Beaujolais de l'année,* i.e., Beaujolais of the current vintage, before Christmas, and a number of bistros are as well-known for their excellent Beaujolais as for their food. These very young wines are comparatively light-bodied, with neither the character nor the alcoholic content to maintain a long life. The Beaujolais that is sold in this country will rarely be as delicate, because light wines don't travel well. Wines chosen to be bottled for export should be somewhat fuller-flavored and sturdier, although the best examples will naturally maintain the grace and charm of a typical Beaujolais.

The Beaujolais district can be divided roughly into three parts, producing wines entitled to the appellations Beaujolais, Beaujolais-Villages, and the *grands crûs* of Beaujolais. The southern portion produces somewhat lighter wines entitled to call themselves simply Beaujolais. The appellation Beaujolais Supérieur differs from Beaujolais only in that this wine requires an extra degree of alcohol and production per acre is slightly less. The fact is that the minimum alcoholic requirement for Beaujolais Supérieur is 10 percent but almost all the Beaujolais we drink has 12 percent or more. In other words, most of the wine declared by its producers as Beaujolais could equally well be declared Beaujolais Supérieur, yet only 10 percent is so declared. The reason is that Beaujolais Supérieur pays a slightly higher tax, but the wine will not fetch more than a Beaujolais in the market, because it is the same sort of wine. What all this means to the consumer is that there is no essential difference between Beaujolais and Beaujolais Supérieur, both being produced in the less favored part of the Beaujolais district.

The next step up the ladder of *appellation contrôlée* laws for Beaujolais is Beaujolais-Villages. Wines so labeled come from about thirty-five towns in the center of the region, whose vineyards consistently produce better wines than those farther south. Occasionally the actual village name will appear on the label, but as these are not at all known here, the wines are usually labeled simply as Beaujolais-Villages. Interestingly, the law requires the same alcoholic minimum (10 percent) and the same production-per-acre limitations (about two hundred cases per acre) as for Beaujolais Supérieur. The difference, then, is entirely in the soil. About 25 percent of all Beaujolais is entitled to be called Beaujolais-Villages.

The finest of all Beaujolais comes from nine villages in the northernmost part of the region. These nine *grands crûs* are Moulin-à-Vent, Fleurie, Brouilly, Côte de Brouilly, Morgon, Saint-Amour, Chénas, Juliénas, and Chiroubles. These villages produce the wines with the most distinction, their wines are longer-lived, and the price is somewhat higher than for a simple Beaujolais. As these wines are often labeled with only the name of the village, without the word Beaujolais, it pays to remember them if you are looking for something special from the district. Each wine has its special characteristics and its devotees, and these *grands crûs* are among the most agreeable wines found anywhere.

The Beaujolais *crûs* account for about one-quarter of all Beaujolais in an average year, and of the nine villages, Brouilly, Morgon, Moulin-à-Vent, and Fleurie alone produce 75 percent of the total. Moulin-à-Vent is probably the best known of them all, as its wines are considered the sturdiest and longest-lived. Although a Moulin-à-Vent doesn't have the power or depth of a wine from the Côte de Nuits, it does have considerably more character than the typical Beaujolais and can be served with more robust foods. One of the reasons that there is so much Moulin-à-Vent produced is that most of the wines of the neighboring villages of Chénas and Romanèche-Thorins are also entitled to be sold as Moulin-à-Vent.

Fleurie and Brouilly produce lighter and more elegant wines, with an enchanting perfumed bouquet. Although it might be imagined that Côte de Brouilly is a lesser appellation than Brouilly (as is the case with Beaune and Côte de Beaune), the opposite is in fact the case. Côte de Brouilly is an inner appellation reserved for wines made from the slopes of the little hill of Brouilly. Morgon produces a very sturdy wine that needs some bottle age before it's ready to drink. Although the crop is comparatively large, the wine is not often seen in this country.

Juliénas and Chénas both have a rather distinctive *goût de terroir,* or taste of the soil, that sets them apart from their neighbors. Juliénas can be found here, but most of the production of Chénas is legally sold as Moulin-à-Vent. The wines of Saint-Amour, despite its romantic name, are not often exported to the United States, nor are those of Chiroubles. Of the two, Chiroubles is generally a more attractive and distinctive wine.

Beaujolais is made by thousands of small producers, most of whom sell their wine in barrel to local shippers. About one-third of all the Beaujolais produced, from the simplest wines to the best *crûs,* come from the eighteen cooperative cellars in the region. There are also a number of larger domains that produce hundreds of barrels annually from their extensive vineyards. Occasionally, the name of a particular vineyard appears on a Beaujolais label—and some of these are quite good—but Beaujolais is a region where individual vineyards are not nearly as important a guide to quality as in Bordeaux or along the Rhine, for example.

In sum, the wines of Beaujolais vary from rather light and fragile wines to the richer and fuller wines of some of the *crûs.* There is naturally a tremendous choice, but it is a sad fact that there is much more Beaujolais drunk than is produced in the vineyards themselves. A Beaujolais selling for much under two dollars will rarely have the delightful characteristics of a true Beaujolais, and unfortunately many beginning drinkers have formed their opinion of Beaujolais on rather disappointing examples. For a little more money ($2.50 to $3.50) you can get a Beaujolais-Villages or, better yet, a wine from one of the *grand crû* villages, and the difference in quality will often be dramatic. Remember that when you taste Beaujolais you are looking for fruit rather than for the depth of flavor and complexity that are the characteristics of a fine Bordeaux or Burgundy. Beaujolais tastes best at cellar temperature (55 to 60°F) and you might try putting a bottle on the bottom shelf of the refrigerator for fifteen or twenty minutes to cool it down slightly. The wine tastes all the fresher and seems even more delightful.

THE RHÔNE VALLEY

The Rhône River joins the Saône at Lyons and continues south, reaching the sea near Marseilles. The wines of the Côtes du Rhône come from vineyards planted on both banks of the Rhône, starting about twenty miles south of Lyons at Vienne and continuing 120 miles to Avignon. About 95 percent of Rhône wines are red, but the region includes a famous rosé—Tavel—and some unusual white wines.

The hot and sunny climate typical of the Rhône Valley produces red wines that are—at their best—more robust and less elegant than the wines of Burgundy. The lesser wines are, in general, fuller flavored and less perfumed than, say, the wines of Beaujolais, whose vineyards begin just north of Lyons. The climate along this part of the Rhône is generally more dependable than in other parts of France, and does not always correspond to conditions in Bordeaux and Burgundy. For example, 1960 was a better vintage in the Rhône than was 1959, while the reverse was generally true in the rest of the French vineyards. The intense heat here produces wines that contain more alcohol (and hence more body) than in more northerly vineyards, and this is reflected in the minimums set by the *appellation contrôlée* laws. Whereas 9 percent is required for Beaujolais and 10 percent for Beaujolais *crûs* such as Moulin-à-Vent, the legal minimum for Côtes du Rhône is 10.5 percent and for Châteauneuf-du-Pape, 12.5 percent.

The appellation Côtes du Rhône is the lowest common denominator for the region, and production is abundant—about ten million cases, 99 percent of it red. An inexpensive Côtes du Rhône is a wine without much character or distinction, but it can be a dependable everyday red wine. There are five villages producing somewhat better wines, whose names can be appended on a label to the regional appellation Côtes du Rhône. Of these, Gigondas is known for its red wines and Chusclan for its rosé.

The most famous of all the Rhône wines comes from Châteauneuf-du-Pape, a village located about ten miles from Avignon. A few thousand cases a year of white Châteauneuf-du-Pape are produced—the wine is distinctive and full-flavored—but it is for its red wines that the village is world famous. The name comes from a now ruined castle, built in the fourteenth century as a summer house for Pope Clement V. During most of the fourteenth century the popes were French, and Avignon replaced Rome as the papal seat. The summer residence was called Châteauneuf, or new castle, to distinguish it from the existing papal fortress in Avignon. It was at this time that vines were first planted in the district. When the castle was destroyed two centuries later, the vineyards went untended until the nineteenth century. At that time the wines of Châteauneuf-du-Pape were reintroduced to Parisian society, and the wine has now established itself as one of the best-known red wines in the world.

Wine-makers have discovered over the years that the intense heat of the Rhône Valley does not favor the growth of any of the finest grape varieties. Instead, a number of different varieties are used, each one contributing a particular characteristic to the finished wine. In Châteauneuf-du-Pape, a dozen grape varieties are permitted, and some growers claim that they should all be used to produce the finest wines. Different growers plant their vineyards in different proportions, because one variety will produce more wine per acre, while another makes the most robust wines, and so on, meaning that the wines of Châteauneuf-du-Pape will vary from domain to domain. This variation in wine is further affected by the different vinification methods used in the district. Châteauneuf-du-Pape has long been known as a wine that needs several years of bottle age to reach maturity, and a number of growers continue to employ the long vatting and long maturation in barrel that produces long-lived wines. At the same time, the increasing demand for well-known wines throughout the world, and the eagerness of the consumer to drink good vintages as soon as they are available, has caused a number of domains to vinify their Châteauneuf-du-Pape more in the manner of Beaujolais, to produce a full-bodied but relatively fast-maturing wine that will be ready to drink sooner. In other words, you should be willing to experiment among the different shippers and domains to find the kind of characteristics you prefer. Although Châteauneuf-du-Pape is rarely an exciting wine, it is both dependable and widely available, and these are factors in its favor.

About eight miles on the other side of Avignon is Tavel, which produces what many people consider the finest rosé of France. Made primarily from the Grenache grape, the wine is dry, has a most attractive and distinctive pink-orange hue, and is certainly the rosé with the most character and balance. Only two hundred thousand cases or so are made annually, and a great deal of that comes from the Cooperative of Tavel, although it goes to market under various names. There are, as well, a number of large domains producing estate-bottled Tavel.

Close to Tavel is the village of Lirac, known primarily for its rosé, similar in style to that of Tavel, but less well-known.

Châteauneuf-du-Pape, Tavel, and the regional appellation Côtes du Rhône are the best-known names of the district, and these wines account for almost all the sales in this country of Rhône Valley wines. There are, however, some interesting wines produced in the northern half of the region, and they are worth a quick look.

Condrieu is a white wine, soft and flowery, with a bouquet reminiscent of peaches. More famous is the little vineyard of Château Grillet, whose wine is similar to Condrieu. Its fame is largely based on the fact that this vineyard produces only two hundred cases a year, a great deal of it sold at the world-famous La Pyramide restaurant in nearby Vienne.

Côte Rotie is a big-bodied red wine that is occasionally seen here. The slopes of Hermitage produce red and white wines, both quite rich in flavor. Crozes-Hermitage is a recently established appellation for red and white wines coming from vineyards fanning out from those of Hermitage itself. Crozes-Hermitage produces almost three times as much wine as Hermitage, and its wines are thought to be somewhat less distinctive than those of Hermitage.

THE LOIRE VALLEY

The Loire is famous to tourists for its historic châteaux and for a variety of agreeable and inexpensive wines produced along its banks. But although the châteaux of the Loire are centered around Tours, the wines of the Loire Valley are produced along most of its 650-mile course. About three-quarters of the wines produced along the Loire are white, and a certain amount of agreeable and popular rosé is made. A small amount of red wine is also produced, although the red wines are not so easily found in this country. If the Loire Valley produces no great wines (with the possible exception of some sweet dessert wines that are rarely exported), it does produce quite a variety of delightful wines that are becoming increasingly popular here because of their relatively modest cost. All of the whites and rosés can be—and should be—consumed young.

Starting at Nantes at the mouth of the Loire, the first wine district is Muscadet. This appellation is atypical of French wine names as it is not the name of a village, but of the grape variety used to make the dry white wines of the region. The Muscadet grape, brought from Burgundy in the sixteenth century, was extensively planted and ultimately gave its name to the vineyard region around Nantes. American wine drinkers may have been put off at first by its name, similar to that of the sweet Muscatel wines produced from the Muscat grape, to which Muscadet bears no relationship whatsoever. There is nearly as much wine produced annually in Muscadet as in Beaujolais, which explains why the wine is found so frequently in Paris restaurants and why it is not expensive in this country, the price being around $2.50 a bottle. In the past a good deal of Muscadet was sold as Chablis, which gives you some indication of its taste, although this refreshing wine is somewhat lighter and more tart. Nantes is the capital of Brittany, a region famous for its shellfish, and Muscadet is a perfect accompaniment to seafood, a first course, or lighter foods in general.

The best examples of Muscadet come from the Sèvre-et-Maine district, and these words will be found on the label. Rather than being an inner appellation, however, Sèvre-et-Maine produces about 70 percent of all Muscadet, so most of the wines imported here come from this district. You may also occasionally find a bottle labeled Muscadet *sur lie,* or on the lees. This wine is prized by some connoisseurs as an especially delightful example of Muscadet, because it means that the wine has been bottled very early and directly from the barrel while still resting on its lees, or natural deposits.

The next wine city up the Loire is Angers, which has given its name to the district of Anjou. The best known of the Anjou wines is, of course, Anjou Rosé. This light, mellow, and agreeable wine is made from a lesser grape variety, the Groslot. The relative sweetness of the wine depends on the shipper's specifications, although none of the Anjou rosés on the market are dry. A second rosé is Anjou Rosé de Cabernet, made from the famous red wine grape of Bordeaux. This wine is less sweet and has somewhat more character than does Anjou Rosé.

The Anjou district also produces white wines ranging in character from fairly dry to quite sweet and rich. The wines are made from the Chenin Blanc grape, known locally along the Loire as the Pineau de la Loire, although it is not related to the Pinot Blanc of Burgundy. The three main producing areas are the Côteaux de la Loire, the Côteaux de l'Aubance, and the Côteaux du Layon, the Aubance and the Layon being tributaries of the Loire. The Côteaux du Layon produces by far the most wine—mellow and rounded in character—but it is hard to find here. The wines produced in Quarts de Chaume and Bonnezeaux are especially rich and luscious wines that are considered by local partisans to rival the best châteaux of Sauternes.

The village of Saumur produces white wines from the Chenin Blanc and rosés and red from the Cabernet Franc. The reds are attractive, especially those from the village of Champigny. If you come across a bottle of Saumur de Champigny, it's well worth trying.

The city of Tours is the one most familiar to tourists, as it is here that most of the historic châteaux are found. Chambord, Azay-le-Rideau, Chenonceaux, and Amboise (where Leonardo da Vinci is buried) are among the most famous. Unfortunately, most of the Touraine wines are of minor interest and consumed locally. The most famous exception is the wine of Vouvray, a village ten miles from Tours. The town is noted for its chalk hills, and its inhabitants have dug caves into the slopes that are used both as wine cellars and homes. A number of the houses built along the slopes are mere façades with the greater part of these homes situated within the hillsides themselves.

We know Vouvray in the United States as a pleasant and fairly dry white wine, but if you visit the local cellars, you'll discover that Vouvray can be very dry, mellow, or quite sweet, and that it can be still, *pétillant,* that is, slightly sparkling, or fully sparkling like Champagne. The Chenin Blanc grape is used to make Vouvray and in sunny years it produces a most attractive mellow wine; when there is less sunshine, the wine will be drier in taste. In recent years, however, the trend here and elsewhere toward drier wines has encouraged the Vouvray wine-makers to alter their vinification so that their wines are completely fermented out to produce a dry wine. As for the rich dessert wines, they are carefully produced in exceptionally sunny years, and a visit to a local shipper or grower will often end with a bottle of ten- or twenty-year-old sweet Vouvray.

Vouvray is also known for its *mousseux,* or sparkling wines, made by the Champagne process. The *pétillant* wines are those that are bottled before fermentation is complete, so that a certain amount of sparkle is produced in the corked bottle, giving the wine a pleasant crackling quality. Unfortunately, United States tax laws on all sparkling wines make sparkling and *pétillant* Vouvray comparatively expensive.

Across the river from Vouvray is Mountlouis, whose

wines are similar to those of Vouvray, though perhaps not quite as good.

The Touraine also produces two red wines in the villages of Chinon and Bourgueil. Rabelais was born in Chinon, and he often sang the praises of his local wine and of wine in general. Made from the Cabernet grape, these two wines nevertheless have the refreshing qualities of a good Beaujolais, but with somewhat more character. The best wines of Bourgueil come from the adjoining village of Saint-Nicolas-de-Bourgueil, and its wines are so labeled.

Up the Loire past Orleans, and just before Nevers, are two villages that produce the best white wines of the Loire Valley—Sancerre and Pouilly-sur-Loire. Although we know the hamlet of Sancerre for its wines, it is as famous to the French for its goat cheese. Many of the wine growers also maintain a herd of goats, and they serve their homemade cheeses with as much pride as their wines. The wines of Sancerre are not abundant, but they have a distinctive character that has established their reputation in Paris and, now, in this country. The wine is made from the Sauvignon Blanc grape that is used to make the dry white wines of Bordeaux, but it takes on a completely different character in Sancerre—very dry, full-flavored, and with an attractive tang. For this reason Sancerre is a good wine to serve with robust dishes that call for a white wine: unlike the delicate wines of Muscadet, this wine can hold its own with rich foods.

The growers of Sancerre have also planted part of their vineyards with the Pinot Noir grape, and they make small quantities of very agreeable rosé and red wines.

The village of Pouilly-sur-Loire produces two wines. The Chasselas grape (well-known in Switzerland as the Fendant) produces a wine labeled, appropriately enough, Pouilly-sur-Loire. This is an agreeable country wine that is not often seen here, and which is at its best within a year of the vintage. The village also produces in greater quantity a wine from the Sauvignon Blanc grape, locally known as the Blanc Fumé, or Smoky White (there are various explanations, none of them definitive). The correct name of this wine is Blanc Fumé de Pouilly-sur-Loire, to distinguish it from a Pouilly-sur-Loire. As it happens, a number of potential customers here and elsewhere, seeing the words

Pouilly-sur-Loire on the label, incorrectly assumed that the lesser wine was being palmed off on them. The name was thus shortened to Pouilly-Fumé, an unusual appellation for France, as the village and grape name are combined. This, in turn, has led many people to confuse Pouilly-Fumé from the Loire with Pouilly-Fuissé from southern Burgundy, made from the Chardonnay grape. In any event, Pouilly-Fumé is seen increasingly on restaurant wine lists (occasionally under White Burgundy) and its rich flavor—less elegant than a good Pouilly-Fuissé, but seemingly drier—makes it a good all-purpose accompaniment to food.

The white wines of Quincy and Reuilly are also considered Loire wines, although these towns are actually situated along the Cher, a tributary of the Loire. The wines have a crisp, dry taste similar to those of Sancerre and Pouilly-Fumé.

ALSACE, PROVENCE, AND OTHER WINES

The hillside vineyards of Alsace are among the most beautiful in all of France, and the area is dotted with delightful little villages of the kind that are used as illustrations in children's storybooks. France is separated from Germany here by the Rhine, but the vineyards of Alsace are set back from the river's edge and lie along the slopes of the Vosges Mountains. Alsace produces a tremendous amount of refreshing white wines (and a minuscule amount of undistinguished red wines), which complement perfectly the rich cuisine of the region with its *foie gras,* sauerkraut dishes, and sausages.

Between 1870 and 1914 Alsace, and the neighboring province of Lorraine, were part of Germany. At the time, Germany did not want Alsatian wines to compete with her own Rhine and Moselle wines and encouraged the production of cheap, inferior wines, much of which was used in the manufacture of Sekt, German sparkling wines. After World War I, the growers of Alsace realized that their best chance of commercial success would be with finer wines, and they set about replanting their vineyards with the better grape varieties.

Alsace is unique in France in that its wines are labeled with the name of the grape used to make the wine, rather than with the village or vineyard from which the wine comes. In 1962 Alsace was at last granted *appellation contrôlée* status, based on the continued use of varietal names. Alsace is probably the only *appellation contrôlée* region that does not have specific quantity controls, and the yield per acre in good vintages is abundant. Alsace produces almost ten million cases of wine in a good year, making it the white wine region second only to Bordeaux in all of France. Although the better Alsatian wines are readily available in this country, they have not yet become popular and less than 1 percent of all French wines imported into the United States are Alsatian.

The names you will most often find on a bottle of Alsatian wine are Gewürztraminer, Traminer, Riesling, Sylvaner, and, occasionally, Tokay d'Alsace. The most distinctive of these wines is the Gewürztraminer. With its highly perfumed bouquet, pungent and spicy flavor, it is one of the most unusual and individual wines found anywhere. It can be argued that the Riesling is a more distinguished grape producing a wine with greater breed, but it has always seemed to me that it is the Gewürztraminer, with its unique personality, that sets off Alsatian wines from those of the rest of France, and from the German vineyards farther down the Rhine. The wine is made from the Traminer grape: the most successful examples of Traminer in a particular vintage are set aside to be bottled as Gewürztraminer, or spicy Traminer. Wines labeled Traminer are simply less pungent examples of this wine.

The Riesling, the outstanding white wine grape of the German vineyards, produces less flowery and somewhat drier wines in Alsace, with perhaps more body and character. The Sylvaner is not considered a noble grape, but the best examples from Alsace are very agreeable and refreshing, and are usually good value both on the retail shelf and on restaurant wine lists. The Tokay d'Alsace is a local name for a pleasant white wine made from the Pinot Gris. It bears no relation to the sweet, rich Tokay of Hungary, made in a special way from the Furmint grape.

You will sometimes find certain bottles of Alsatian wine bearing the words *grand vin, grand crû,* or *grande reserve.*

These are legally defined guarantees that the wine has met slightly higher standards of quality.

Because Alsace is often identified with Germany and because Alsatian wines are marketed in the same sloping bottles that are used for German wines, they are often compared, unfairly, to the wines of the Rhine and Moselle. Alsatian wines may never achieve the particular style of the best German estates, but they are sound and dependable wines and even the best of them are not expensive.

The Alsatian wines found in the United States are known by brand names, because it is the shippers, rather than individual domains, that control the Alsace wine trade. Alsace is quite unusual among French wine districts in that most of the growers either bring their grapes to cooperative cellars or else sell them directly to the large shipping houses, rather than vinifying the wine themselves. In other words, the shippers do not only buy wine but also grapes at the time of the vintage, and can then vinify the wines from each grape variety to their own specifications. Thus Alsatian shippers have much more control over the wines they sell than do shippers in other French viticultural districts (except for Champagne, where the same arrangement prevails).

Provence

The region of Provence extends along the Mediterranean coast from Marseilles east to Nice. This 120-mile stretch is dotted with fishing villages and with such famous resorts as Saint-Tropez, Cannes, Antibes, and Juan-les-Pins. Many vacationers have probably had their first, and perhaps their most pleasant, vinous experiences while relaxing in the sun. A holiday mood and a seafood lunch on a terrace overlooking the water can add a great deal of enchantment to the agreeable rosés of Provence, and it is disappointing to discover that these wines never taste quite the same when consumed at home. It's true that many of these delicate and charming wines served in carafes do not travel well, but then neither does the mood in which they were first enjoyed. Of the vast amount of wine produced in this part of France, mostly for local consumption, there is a certain amount that stands out from the rest. The best wines are entitled to the V.D.Q.S. appellation Côtes de Provence. The V.D.Q.S. wines are just a rank below those of *appellation contrôlée* standards, but the same kind of rules apply: specified grape varieties, minimum alcoholic content, delimited production areas, and so forth. Most of the Côtes de Provence wines are rosé, and their labels carry the little official stamp of V.D.Q.S. quality. A number of large domains have made an effort to expand their export market, and these Provence wines are noted for their fancy bottles and distinctively designed labels.

The seacoast villages of Bandol and Cassis each produce red, white, and rosé wines that are entitled to *appellation contrôlée* status. Bandol produces mostly reds and rosés—dry wines with a fairly well-defined character. Cassis is known primarily for its white wine, full-flavored and a favorite accompaniment to the local *bouillabaisse*. The wines of Cassis bear no relation to the Cassis made in Dijon. The latter is a black-currant syrup used on desserts and to flavor certain drinks, notably white wine and cassis, a popular Burgundian aperitif.

Other Wines

Near the Swiss border, not far from Geneva, two white wines are produced that are occasionally seen in this country. Crépy, made a few miles from the lake of Geneva, is a light dry wine made from the Chasselas grape. Being a wine made in the mountains near Switzerland and from a grape widely grown there, it's no surprise that Crépy resembles a Swiss wine. Seyssel is a white wine from the Haute-Savoie, but most of its production is transformed, by the Champagne process, into a *mousseux*. Sparkling Seyssel is well-known to skiers at nearby Mégève and Chamonix and is occasionally found in this country as well.

The vast area of the Midi in the south of France produces tremendous amounts of ordinary wine and is by far the largest viticultural area in the country. Most of this wine is totally anonymous and is used to make the commercial blends sold within France. There are a few districts, however, whose soil produces wines consistently distinguishable from those of their neighbors, and these are entitled to the V.D.Q.S. appellation. About the only one seen in this country is the red wine from Corbières, a sturdy wine similar to a good Côtes du Rhône.

The Jura district, east of Burgundy, produces a limited amount of red, white, and rosé wines, of which Arbois rosé is the one most often seen in Paris. There are also a few thousand cases a year produced of a very special white wine, Château-Chalon, made in a rather unusual way. After fermentation, the wine is aged for several years in small barrels that are not completely filled, thus exposing the wine to air. The resulting oxidation causes a yeast film to form, similar to that produced in certain Sherries by a similar exposure, and the finished wine is known as a *vin jaune*. As you would expect, Château-Chalon is a most curious white wine, similar to a dry Sherry, but with perhaps more bouquet and a more complex flavor.

The Wines of
Germany

By world standards, Germany is not one of the major
wine-producing nations. Its annual production is less than
10 percent that of France, and California produces nearly
as much table wine. Vines are planted in only a small section of the country, and wine is not the national beverage
of Germany as it is of France and Italy: beer is the
German's daily drink. Despite all this, Germany produces
what are acknowledged to be the greatest white wines in
the world. The Riesling, when planted in the finest vineyards along the Rhine and Moselle, produces a truly superb
wine with an unmistakable and incomparable bouquet and
with extraordinary elegance and breed.

There is less variety to German wines than to those of
most wine-producing nations, and 85 percent of them are
white. (Red wines are made in Baden and Württemberg,
in the Rheinpfalz, along the Ahr, and in the villages of
Assmannshausen and Ingelheim, but they are all too light
to compare favorably with those available from other countries.) All of Germany's white wines, with the possible
exception of the Steinweins from Franconia, bear a family
resemblance: a distinctive, flowery bouquet, and a taste
characterized by a more-or-less harmonious balance of
sweetness and acidity that gives them a distinctive pi-
quancy. Nevertheless, there are many consumers who will-
ingly experiment with wines from different countries, but
who reject all German wines as too sweet. It's true that even
the driest and liveliest examples of Rhines and Moselles
will never have the full-bodied dryness of, say, a good
white Burgundy. But German wines have instead a charm

and appeal unequaled by any other wines, and the best of them have an extraordinary richness of bouquet and flavor that has established their outstanding reputation. Undoubtedly, many people are put off by the seeming complexity of German wine labels, with their unfamiliar and unpronounceable names, often made even less legible by the use of Gothic script. Consequently, most sales in this country consist of two wines with generic names, Liebfraumilch and Moselblümchen, plus a few regional names such as Piesporter, Bernkasteler, Niersteiner, and Rüdesheimer. These wines exist at all prices, and the cheapest ones can only hint at the bouquet and ripeness that characterize German wines, without in any way suggesting their potential refinement and complexity.

Curiously enough, consumers who are aware of at least the names of the best vineyards of Bordeaux and Burgundy often have no parallel knowledge of the best vineyards of the Rhine or Moselle. A wine drinker who will occasionally spend a bit more to try a famous French, Italian, or California wine feels lost when it comes to German wines and will at best simply buy a more expensive regional wine. It is, of course, at the level of the top vineyards and most famous domains that the best German wines are to be found, but American unfamiliarity with their names, perhaps coupled with the discouraging experience of a cheap Liebfraumilch, seems unfortunately to have made these outstanding wines less accessible to the American palate. My own experience is that anyone to whom a good German wine has been offered has invariably expressed amazement that wines of this style and caliber existed.

German wine labels, which appear so confusing at first glance, are in fact the most specific wine labels in the world for the best wines. For less good wines more is communicated by what is left off than by what is stated. The new German wine laws, which went into effect with the 1971 vintage, should have an important effect on the quality of regional wines. Because there is a considerable difference in the nomenclature of German labels for wines made before 1971 and those made since, the consumer will have to keep two systems of labeling in mind when looking at German labels for the next few years, while older wines are still available. In order to understand all the informa-

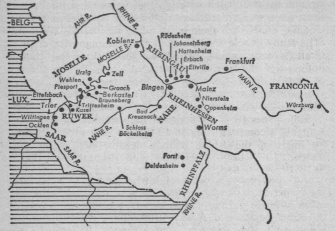

The German Wine Districts

tion that is contained on German labels, it is first necessary to examine some of the elements that enter into the making of German wines.

The German vineyards extend up to, and even slightly beyond, what is known as the northern limit of the vine. Farther north, excessively cold winters will kill the vines, and summers lacking in adequate sunshine would prevent grapes from properly ripening. The best wines are made on slopes and steep hillsides facing south, where their height and direction enable the grapes to catch the maximum amount of sunshine. The poor soil that characterizes these vineyards is unsuitable for any other crop, and the steep incline of many vineyards makes it impossible to use modern machinery. It is by hand labor of thousands of growers that these vines are tended, and it's only because the wines produced can be so superb (and expensive) that it remains commercially worthwhile for these vineyards to be cultivated. (Actually, until the eighteenth century, most German wines were red.) There are over ninety thousand growers tending their own vines in Germany, and 85 percent of them own less than four acres. Less than 1 percent own more than twenty acres, but it is to a large extent among these larger domains that the most famous wine-producing names are found.

The Rhine is the informing river of German viticulture, and all German wines are produced either along the Rhine or along the banks of its many tributaries. The principal wine regions along the Rhine itself are the Rheinpfalz, or Palatinate, known for its soft, full, rounded wines; the Rheinhessen, which produces a tremendous quantity of agreeable wines (it is the home of Liebfraumilch); and the Rheingau, a comparatively small district that produces the very finest of the Rhine wines—elegant, rich, and well balanced. The Moselle (which has two tributaries, the Saar and the Ruwer) joins the Rhine at Koblentz: its wines are light-bodied, fragrant, and possess a refreshing crispness derived from their acidity. The Nahe joins the Rhine at Bingen, and despite its geographical position halfway between the Rhine and Moselle, its best wines have the richness and style of the best of the Rhine wines.

The vineyards of Franconia, along the Main, produce wines quite different from those of the Rhine and Moselle, and less often seen here. These drier wines have less bouquet and more body, and a distinctive earthy taste. Franconia wines, sometimes referred to generically as Steinweins after its most famous single vineyard, are easy to spot because they are always shipped in the distinctive *Bocksbeutel*, a squat, rounded bottle similar to that often used for Chilean wines.

The two German states of Baden and Württemberg also produce a substantial amount of wine, much of it red. The white wines, rarely imported here, include very little Riesling and are similar in style to the wines of Alsace.

Except for the wines of Franconia, just about all other German wines are sold in slender tapering bottles—Rhine wines in brown bottles, Moselles in pale green. This distinction can be of help in remembering their general characteristics: the richer, fuller, deeper flavor of the Rhines, and the fresher, more graceful, and lighter-colored wines of the Moselle.

Nowhere in the world is the old adage more relevant—that the vine flourishes best where conditions are most difficult—than along the Rhine and Moselle. It is here that the Riesling has demonstrated why it is considered one of the half-dozen classic grape varieties for the production of outstanding wine. Elsewhere—in Switzerland, Austria, Alsace, California—wines made from this grape will have some of the fruit and style for which it is known, but never to the same degree. Unfortunately, the Riesling flowers early, and is susceptible to the spring frosts that sometimes harm a year's crop. It also ripens late, and a vintage that takes place in October or November is subject to cold, rain, early winter frosts, and even snow. Finally, the Riesling has a small yield. Nevertheless, its quality is such that most of the vineyards of the Moselle and of the Rheingau are planted in Riesling, as are the best vineyards in the Rheinhessen and Rheinpfalz.

The Sylvaner flowers later and bears fruit sooner, but its wines lack the distinction and breed of which the Riesling is capable (except occasionally in the Rheinhessen). It is the dominant grape in Germany, especially in the Rheinhessen, Rheinpfalz, and Franconia.

The Traminer, famous in Alsace, is not widely planted in Germany and is much less frequently seen than certain sturdier vines, notably the Müller-Thurgau. This is a cross between the Riesling and Sylvaner that ripens more quickly (and therefore more safely) and gives a higher yield. Its wines are sound and pleasant, but they age fairly quickly and are mostly used in regional blends.

A harvest of fully ripened grapes can not be taken for granted in Germany as it can, say, in the Côtes du Rhône, California, or Italy. For this reason vintages along the Rhine and Moselle are more complicated, and this is reflected in the nature of the wines produced and the way they are labeled. In the first place, in every wine-producing community, the village council determines each year the exact date at which the grapes will have achieved a minimum degree of ripeness before which no grapes can be harvested. Guards are posted in the vineyards (they are also responsible for scaring away birds that try to eat the grapes) and the vintage begins on the prearranged day. Most of the grapes are picked and brought back to the press rooms, wineries, and cooperative cellars, as in any wine-making region. In certain years, however, some growers may decide to wait an additional two or three weeks before picking some of their vines, so that additional sunshine will ripen these grapes more fully. The resulting wine is known as Spätlese, or late picking, and it will be fuller, rounder, somewhat richer than the normal wine from the same vineyard. A grower may also decide to vinify separately the very ripest bunches on the vines, and such wines are known as Auslese, or selected picking. Technically speaking, an Auslese does not have to be picked as late as a Spätlese, and in fact the vintagers carry baskets with special compartments in which they can put grapes of Auslese quality. These especially ripe grapes will make a wine even richer and more luscious than a Spätlese, and more expensive.

Several steps higher in quality and scarcity are wines known as Beerenauslese, or selected berry picking: here individual berries that are unusually ripe are put aside to make a sweet and fragrant wine. Finally, the pinnacle of this hierarchy are wines made from overripe grapes that have been attacked by a special mold, known as *pourriture noble* in Sauternes and Barsac, and as *Edelfäule* in Germany. These shriveled grapes will have a much higher proportion of natural sugar, and the resulting wine, which is very difficult to ferment, is the most extraordinary nectar that a vineyard can produce. It is very sweet, of course, but with a balancing acidity and harmony that make it absolutely unique. It is called Trockenbeerenauslese, i.e., the selected picking of dried shriveled berries, and it is only produced in outstanding years and in minute quantities. Vintages in the northerly climate of the German vineyards are precarious enough, and to leave grapes out to ripen for weeks after the normal harvest, counting on additional sunny days to produce wines of Spätlese quality and better, is naturally a risk that not every vineyard owner is prepared to take. As a general indication of the comparative value of this progression of wines in a given vineyard, a normal vineyard wine might sell for $3.50; Spätlese for $4.25; Auslese for $5.00; Beerenauslese for $20.00 to $25.00; and the Trockenbeerenauslese for $35.00 to $60.00.

While on the subject of rare wines, there are two other special indications that you may come across on an expensive bottle. Edelbeerenauslese indicates that this particular Beerenauslese is, in the producer's opinion, of exceptional quality: *edel* means noble. An Eiswein, or ice wine, is made from fully ripe grapes of at least Spätlese quality that have been frozen on the vine. The resulting juice will naturally be concentrated in its qualities, and the quantity greatly reduced. Ice wines are not usually produced in years that can produce a Trockenbeerenauslese, as the latter requires a long sunny fall with some moisture to start the noble rot, whereas ice wines require sunshine followed by a frost.

In most of the world's vineyard districts, a good vintage is one in which the grapes ripen fully and the resulting dry wine is complete, with a proper degree of alcohol. In Germany, the best vintages are those in which the grapes are not only ripe, but overripe, so that there is enough grape sugar present to produce some top wines that will be rich and sweet. German wine-makers describe the nature of a vintage in terms of the Oechsle degree (sugar content) of the must, or unfermented grape juice. They are concerned not only with determining how much alcohol a certain amount of sugar will produce during fermentation, but also whether there is enough sugar present to produce a wine with sufficient alcohol plus the residual sugar needed to make a fine Spätlese or Auslese.

It's only in the last one hundred years that German wines have been labeled with their exact place of origin: until then they were exported under broad regional names. In Shakespeare's day, people drank Rhenish, although that was probably a red wine. More recently the English referred to all Rhine wines as Hocks, probably derived from the town of Hochheim, from which these wines were shipped to England. To this day, many English wine lists refer to German wines as Hocks and Moselles.

German wine labels can be the most specific in the world. As a start, you will be told the vintage, the village and specific vineyard from which the wine has come, the grape variety, and the conditions under which the grapes were picked.

1959 Forster Jesuitengarten Riesling Spätlese

The first word is the village, Forst, and a wine from there is a Forster (as a man from London is a Londoner); Jesuitengarten is the specific vineyard; the wine was made from the Riesling, and was picked after the normal harvest (Spätlese). There are a few exceptions to this rule of village and vineyard: vineyards so famous that their names stand alone on a label without that of their respective villages. Among such vineyards are Schloss Johannisberg, Schloss Vollrads, Steinberg, and Scharzhofberg.

When you look at a German wine label, then, you can quickly tell just where it comes from and more-or-less how rich and sweet the wine will be. There are two things you should know at this point. There are perhaps fifty thousand vineyard names in Germany (considerably reduced by the new wine laws) and many of them repeat themselves in various districts. For the most part they are not proper names, nor derived etymologically from other languages, as in Bordeaux and Burgundy, but rather picturesque descriptive names. Jesuitengarten may be translated as Garden of the Jesuits. Other typical names mean Little Rose Garden, Michael's Hill, Green House, Church Path, High Acre, and so forth. German labels take on a more colorful and less complex aspect if you can figure out some of these names, and you can expect to see many combinations of the same words reappearing in different districts. A specific vineyard plot in Germany is called a *Lage,* which corresponds to a *crû* in Bordeaux.

The other thing you must know is that the name of the grape does not always appear on the label. It is taken for granted by grower and consumer that the wine from every good vineyard in the Moselle and in the Rheingau is made exclusively from the Riesling grape. For this reason many of the best bottles do not indicate Riesling anywhere on the label, although some of them will. The best vineyards in the Rheinhessen and Rheinpfalz, however, will always state on their labels the fact that a given wine comes from the Riesling, because those regions are planted mostly in Sylvaner and Müller-Thurgau. Incidentally, it isn't rare to see a Rheinhessen vineyard wine that proudly states that it is made from the Sylvaner, perhaps even of Spätlese or Auslese quality.

There are some additional words that appear on German labels. *Cabinet* or *Kabinett* derives from a time when proprietors put aside their best wine for special occasions. It is now used as a mark of special quality, and although its meaning has been flexible and determined by each producer, a wine marked *Cabinet* will usually be of at least Spätlese quality. *Feine* or *feinste* (as in *feine Auslese*) is the producer's indication that he believes this to be an exceptionally good cask of the specified wine. As a matter of fact, the number of the actual barrel from which a particular bottle of wine comes will sometimes be found indicated on a label, as *Fass* for Rhine wines, *Fuder* for Moselles.

Although German wine labels appear a little more imposing than those from France, they are not, as you see, so very difficult to read. The problem in getting to know the best German wines is not that the labels are not specific enough, but rather than they are, in a sense, too specific. Stated another way, there are more famous vineyards in Germany than in Bordeaux, more excellent wine villages than in Burgundy, and far more levels of excellence for a given wine than anywhere else in the world. There is no shortcut to even a casual acquaintance with the wine towns and their most famous vineyards, and these will be examined in some detail below, district by district.

There is one other important fact about German vineyards that must be mentioned at this point, which is that their ownership is mostly split, as in Burgundy, rather than in the hands of a single proprietor or syndicate, as in Bordeaux. Consequently, the names of individual growers and of large domains, who may have holdings in several vineyards scattered among three or four villages, must also be taken into consideration when buying German wines. There are a few large domains whose names will appear again and again on any list of German wines. Unlike the typical Burgundian peasant who produces less than a thousand cases of wine from his property, these large domains will often make twenty-five thousand to fifty thousand cases in a good year (although this may include several properties and a variety of quality levels). The owners of these domains include noble families, religious orders, and the German Federal State itself, which owns some of the best vineyards in the country. Among the firms that specialize in estate-bottled German wines are Kendermann and Hallgarten, and many excellent wines are imported by Frank Schoonmaker.

Here are some words that will help in choosing the best of these wines from vintages prior to 1971. *Originalabfüllung* is the equivalent of chateau or estate bottling. *Kellerabzug* and *Kellerabfüllung* only mean cellar bottling and are no guarantee of estate bottling. *Gewächs, Wachstum* or *Creszenz* in front of a man's name is a guarantee that the bottle contains unsugared wine from the particular specified vineyard, but not necessarily that it has been bottled at the property. The new wine laws do away with the phrase *Originalabfüllung* and substitute *Aus eigenem Lesegut* (from our own harvest) or *Erzeugerabfüllung* (bottled by the producer). Shippers who buy and bottle an individual vineyard wine from a specific estate may use the term *Aus dem Lesegut von* (from the harvest of) along with an indication that the wine is shipper bottled.

Finally, a few German words that should not be confused with proper names: *Erben*—heirs, *Freiherr*—baron, *Graf*—count, *Fürst*—prince, *Kellerei*—cellar, and *Weingut*—wine domain.

As often as not, vintages in Germany do not produce grapes sufficiently ripe to be transformed, unaided, into stable and agreeable wines. A lack of sunshine results in grapes that are too acid and deficient in sugar, and the resulting wines would be low in alcohol (and therefore unstable) and unpleasantly tart. German wine laws permit the addition of sugar to the fermenting juice, or must, to the extent that it will result in an alcoholic content equal to what is normally achieved with ripe grapes. This recourse to chaptalization is frequent in Germany and by no means infrequent in Bordeaux and Burgundy. The difference is that German wines made prior to 1971, which have been chaptalized (the German term is *verbessert*), can not be labeled *Natur* or *Naturrein*. Nor can they be labeled as estate bottled, or bear special quality words such as *Cabinet, Gewächs, Wachstum,* and so forth. And of course, Spätlese and Auslese wines can not be produced by the addition of sugar.

The new wine laws now in effect have created three basic categories for German wines: *Tafelwein*—ordinary or current consumption wines, comparable to the nonappellation wines of France; *Qualitätswein*—quality wines from certain classified areas, similar to *appellation contrôlée* wines; and

Qualitätswein mit Prädikat—quality wines "with a predi-
cate," that is, with a specific word (such as Spätlese) indicating especially fine quality. The last category applies to
the best wines: Kabinett, Spätlese, Auslese, Beerenauslese,
Trockenbeerenauslese, and Eiswein. None of these *Prädikat*
wines can be sugared, but it can be assumed that *Qualitätswein* and *Tafelwein* have been sugared—thus *Natur* or
Naturrein is no longer necessary on a label. One advantage
of this for the consumer is that the best estates may now
chaptalize their wine in lesser years to increase their sta-
bility and still produce authentic unblended wines from
specific vineyards: these wines will only be entitled to the
Qualitätswein appellation. In effect, the German growers
now have the same flexibility as a proprietor in Chambertin
or Clos Vougeot, who has always been free to estate bottle
his wine whether or not he has had recourse to chaptalization.

It's obvious that although German wine labels are very
specific this doesn't mean that the subject of German wines
is not complex. To cut through the almost infinite possibilities for taste and quality available in German wines, this
rule of thumb can be formulated: an individual vineyard
wine estate bottled by a reputable grower, will be in the top
rank of German wines, especially if the vintage is a good
recent one. If the wine is of Spätlese quality or higher, so
much the better.

Two basic factors, the impossibility of making fine vineyard wines year after year and the difficulty of picking
one's way through the great number of vineyards and their
respective levels of excellence—specifically labeled though
these wines may be—has not unnaturally led to the dominant role played by the German shippers in the American
market, and to the popularity of a few generic and regional
wine names.

The most popular single wine of Germany is Liebfraumilch, and this name may originally have referred to the
wines produced in the small vineyard belonging to the
Liebfrauenkirche in Worms (approximately on the border
between the Rheinhessen and Rheinpfalz). This generic
name can now be used for wine from along any part of
the Rhine, although most of the production comes from
the Rheinhessen. Liebfraumilch can range in price from

one dollar to five dollars a bottle. Most big shippers market a wine priced at around three dollars, and some will also offer a Superior, Gold Label, and so forth, the highest qualities selling for four dollars or more. Because Liebfraumilch is a name that can mean almost anything, it may seem logical to imagine that one will be as bad as the next. On the contrary, where you have only the shipper's name to guide you, it's much better to rely on those whose reputation is based on giving value for money. If you want a German wine in a restaurant, for example, and no attractive vineyard wines are available, you can rely on Sichel's Blue Nun, Deinhard's Hanns Christof, Valckenberg's Madonna, Langenbach's Meister Krone, Julius Kayser's Glockenspiel, and on the Madrigal wines.

Moselblümchen is the Moselle version of Liebfraumilch, and the comparatively lighter wines marketed with that label are just as variable in quality. There are a number of popular German wines labeled to appear to come from individual vineyards, but they are in fact regional wines. These regional wines require some comment, for as their labels get less specific, so do the wine laws controlling them. A wine labeled simply Bernkasteler or Piesporter indicates, by inference, that the wine does not come from a particular vineyard and that it is not made from the Riesling grape. A Bernkasteler Riesling or Johannisberger Riesling, however, suggests a village wine made with Riesling grapes, a step up in quality. Actually, German wine laws for wines at this level are fairly generous. A regional wine with a specific village name can be made from grapes grown within fifteen kilometers (nine miles) in any direction. Because most of these little villages are within a mile or two of each other, this includes a lot of territory. Before the new wine laws came into effect, only two-thirds of the wine had to come from the named village, the named grape, or the named vintage to be so labeled. The new laws have increased the minimum to 75 percent, but more important, they specify that the taste of the wine must be in keeping with its label, and this is to be determined by local tasting panels.

These laws also apply to certain other wines such as Piesporter Michelsberg or Bernkasteler Braunes, whose more specific labeling would suggest that they are the product of an individual vineyard. They are in fact regional wines whose origins are allowed considerable latitude. Among such regional appellations are Urziger Schwarzlay, Niersteiner Fritzenhölle, Hochheimer Daubhaus, Johannisberger Erntebringer, and Eltviller Steinmächer. Once again, the shipper's name is more important here than the name of the wine. Once a label carries any specific indications of quality and authenticity, however, such as *Originalabfüllung* or *Naturrein* on older labels, or *Qualitätswein mit Prädikat* on wines affected by the new laws, the wine is more certain to be just what it says it is.

THE GERMAN WINE DISTRICTS

Rheinpfalz

The Rheinpfalz is the biggest wine-producing district in Germany, and most of its wines are undistinguished and used for current consumption throughout Germany. As the southernmost district in Germany, the Rheinpfalz has a higher proportion of good vintages, and its wines are in general milder, less acid, fuller, and softer. Auslese and Beerenauslese wines are not uncommon in the Pfalz.

The Rheinpfalz vineyards are not actually situated along the Rhine, but on the slopes and fertile plains of the Haardt Mountains, ten or fifteen miles from the river. The Sylvaner is the grape variety most often found here, but the Riesling predominates in the Middle Haardt, the central section that contains the best wine-producing villages: Forst, Deidesheim, Ruppertsberg, and Wachenheim. When choosing wines from this district, it is very helpful to remember that three producers in particular, known as the three B's, are famous for the high quality of their wines: Bassermann-Jordan, Bürklin-Wolf, and von Buhl.

VILLAGE	IMPORTANT VINEYARDS
Forst	Kirchenstück, Jesuitengarten, Ungeheuer
Deidesheim	Leinhöle, Hohenmorgen, Kieselberg.

Rheinhessen

The Rheinhessen begins where the Rheinpfalz leaves off, at Worms, and these two districts account for almost half of the vineyard acreage in Germany. The Rheinhessen produces more wine than the Moselle-Saar-Ruwer and the Rheingau combined. The Sylvaner is the principal grape here, and the bulk of Rheinhessen wines are used to make up shippers' blends, notably Liebfraumilch.

Two villages in the Rheinhessen, Nierstein and Oppenheim, can produce excellent wines from the Riesling grape, but their names are more frequently seen on undistinguished blends. Domtal is a generic name that can be used for any wine from Nierstein, and Niersteiner Domtal is thus the lowest common denominator of wines from this village. However, the best wines from the Rheinhessen, the estate-bottled wines of Spätlese and Auslese quality, are not difficult to find and are quite distinguished.

VILLAGE	IMPORTANT VINEYARDS
Nierstein	Hipping, Auflangen, Rehbach, Orbel
Oppenheim	Sackträger, Herrenberg

Rheingau

The Rheingau is a small district of only six thousand acres, but its wines are, with the very best of the Moselles, the best wines produced in Germany. They are characterized by more body and perhaps more character than those of the Moselle-Saar-Ruwer, whose wines impress more with their grace and delicacy. The Rheingau extends along the Rhine from just past Wiesbaden to Rüdesheim. Beyond Wiesbaden is the village of Hochheim, whose wines are considered as Rheingaus, and beyond Rüdesheim is the village of Assmannshausen, known primarily for its red wines.

The Rheingau contains four vineyards each of whose wines are so outstanding and so famous that its name may appear alone on a label. They are Marcobrunn or Markobrunn, Steinberg, Schloss Vollrads, and Schloss Johannisberg. The Marcobrunn vineyard is located in Erbach and is split among several owners, most of whom actually market the wine as Erbacher Marcobrunn. The other three vineyards are unique in that they are quite large, sixty acres or more, and that each one has but a single owner. Steinberg is owned by the German Federal State, and its wines are made and stored at the twelfth-century monastery nearby, Kloster Eberbach. Schloss Vollrads belongs to the Matuschka-Greiffenclau family, who first settled in Vollrads in the fourteenth centry. Its wines are labeled in ascending order, as *Schlossabzug, Originalabfüllung, Kabinett,* and then Auslese and up. Within each category the bottles are dressed with different colored capsules, each denoting a different level of quality.

Schloss Johannisberg is probably the single most famous vineyard in Germany, and its renown is such that the Riesling grape is known as the Johannisberger in Switzerland, and as the Johannisberg Riesling in California. The vineyard was given to the von Metternich family, its present owners, by the emperor of Austria over 150 years ago, but it was famous long before that. As is the case with Schloss Vollrads, the wines of Schloss Johannisberg are not simply labeled with the usual indications of Spätlese, Auslese, and so forth. There are in fact two different labels used—one shows the family crest, the other a drawing of the property—and each comes in several colors, as do the capsules.

There are, of course, a great many excellent vineyards in the Rheingau besides these four, and in fact the best wines of Rauenthal are often the most expensive of all. Among the most important and most readily found wine families of the Rheingau are Graf Eltz, Langwerth von Simmern, and Graf von Schönborn. The German state is the biggest single owner of vineyards here with over three hundred acres in several villages. Its simple black-and-gold label and the identification *Staatsweinguter* is familiar to everyone who enjoys the best German wines. Here are the most important Rheingau villages and some of their best vineyards.

VILLAGE	IMPORTANT VINEYARDS
Hochheim	Domdechaney, Kirchenstück
Rauenthal	Baiken, Gehrn, Weishell, Wülfen

Eltville	Taubenberg, Sonnenberg, Sandgrube
Erbach	*Marcobrunner* (also *Markobrunner*), Herrenberg, Steinmorgen
Hattenheim	*Steinberger*, Nussbrunnen, Wisselbrunnen, Mannberg
Hallgarten	Deutelsberg, Schönhell, Hendelberg
Winkel	*Schloss Vollrads*, Hasensprung
Johannisberg	*Schloss Johannisberger*, Erntebringer, Klaus
Geisenheim	Rothenberg, Kläuserweg
Rüdesheim	Berg Bronnen, Berg Lay, Berg Rottland

* Vineyard names that appear by themselves on a label are italicized.

Moselle—Saar—Ruwer

Compared to the majestic flow of the Rhine, the erratic path of the Moselle seems frivolous and nowhere more so than in the section known as the Middle Moselle. Yet it is along these steep banks that are found the world-famous wine villages of Piesport, Bernkastel, Wehlen, Zeltingen, Urzig, Graach, and a few others whose names, coupled with that of their best vineyards, identify some of the finest wines to be found anywhere. The Moselle zigzags here to such an extent that the greatest vineyards, always planted so as to face toward the south, are located first on one bank, then on the other. In some cases, the village itself is on the opposite bank, so that these choice slopes can be used entirely for the production of wine. During the vintage, the growers must keep crossing the river to bring the grapes back to their press houses.

The most famous vineyard along the Moselle is Bernkasteler Doctor, which has three owners: the widow of Dr. Thanisch, Deinhard and Company, and the Lauerburg estate. The Thanisch wines are usually combined with those from their part of the Graben vineyard, and sold as Bernkasteler Doctor und Graben. Similarly, the Lauerburg wines are marketed as Bernkasteler Doctor und Bratenhofchen. The firm of Deinhard markets its wine simply as Bernkasteler Doctor. These wines are generally the most expensive of all Moselles, especially those in the Spätlese and Auslese categories.

The Sonnenuhr, or sundial, vineyard of Wehlen is

Bernkasteler Doctor's closest competitor for fame and price. Various members of the Prüm family have holdings in this vineyard. Other families whose names are often to be found on the best bottles of Moselle include Bergweiler, Berres, von Schorlemer, and von Kesselstatt. There are also several hospitals and schools with extensive holdings along the Moselle (as well as the Saar and Ruwer). Names to look for on a label include Bischöfliches Konvikt, Bischöfliches Priesterseminar, Vereinigte Hospitien, St. Nikolaus Hospital, and the Friedrich Wilhelm Gymnasium.

The villages of Zell and Krov have given their names to two popular wines, Zeller Schwarze Katz, or Black Cat, and Krover Nacktarsch, or Bare Bottom, whose labels usually illustrate their names. These are actually generic names and their quality will never be more than acceptable. The vineyard names Bernkasteler Braunes, Graacher Münzlay, Piesporter Michelsberg, and Urziger Schwarzlay, among others, refer to regional blends that can be made from wines produced within several miles of the named village.

Here is a list of the best-known wine-producing villages of the Moselle, and some of their best vineyards.

VILLAGE	IMPORTANT VINEYARDS
Trittenheim	Apotheke, Laurentiusberg
Piesport	Goldtröpfchen, Lay, Taubengarten, Falkenberg
Brauneberg	Juffer, Falkenberg
Bernkastel	Doctor, Badstube, Lay
Graach	Himmelreich, Domprobst, *Josephshofer*
Wehlen	Sonnenuhr, Lay, Klosterlay
Zeltingen	Sonnuhr (or Sonnenuhr), Rotlay, Schlossberg
Urzig	Würzgarten, Kranklay

The Saar and the Ruwer are two tributaries of the Moselle, and their wines are similar in style. Wines from any of the three districts will invariably carry the words Moselle-Saar-Ruwer on their labels. The Saar is the bigger district of the two, and in very good vintages its best wines may outclass those of the Moselle. Saar wines can be superbly elegant at their best, but in lesser vintages they are disappointingly acid and out of balance.

The most famous Saar vineyard, and one of the most famous in Germany, is Scharzhofberg. Located in the village of Wiltingen, the vineyard name stands alone on its distinctive label. Its principal owner is Egon Müller; others are Koch and the Hohe Domkirche, the Cathedral of Trier, which markets its portion as Domscharzhofberger. The Scharzberg vineyard is situated nearby, but its wines are not in the same class as that of Scharzhofberg.

VILLAGE	IMPORTANT VINEYARDS
Serrig	Kupp, Würzburg
Ayl	Herrenberg, Kupp
Ockfen	Bockstein, Geisberg, Herrenberg
Wiltingen	*Scharzhofberger, Scharzberg,* Kupp
Oberemmel	Altenberg, Rosenberg
Kanzem	Altenburg, Sonnenberg

The light, racy wines of the Ruwer are subject to the same peaks and valleys of quality as those of the Saar. The district contains two very famous vineyards, each with a single proprietor. The Maximin Grünhaus vineyard is owned by Count von Schubert, and its best wines are those of the Herrenberg part of the vineyard. In Eitelsbach, the Karthäuserhofberg vineyard is owned by the Rautenstrauch family. Perhaps with a sense of irony, they have devised one of the smallest of all German wine labels to bear this succession of long names.

VILLAGE	IMPORTANT VINEYARDS
Avelsbach	Herrenberg, Altenberg
Kasel	Niesgen, Kehrnagel, Hitzlay
Mertesdorf	*Maximin Grünhauser Herrenberg*
Eitelsbach	Karthäuserhofberg

Nahe

The wines of the Nahe are not very well-known in this country, and even German consumers are less familiar with its best sites. The best of the Nahe wines are very good indeed, and although they are said to combine the best characteristics of the two districts that adjoin it—the Rheingau and the Moselle—they are much closer in style to the best Rheingaus. The best wine-producing villages are Bad Kreuznach (which shortens its name on a label to Kreuznacher), Niederhausen, and Schloss Böckelheim.

Although *Schloss,* or castle, is used in two famous Rheingau vineyard names—Schloss Johannisberg and Schloss Vollrads—Schloss Böckelheim is the name of a village, not a specific vineyard. There is also a Rüdesheim on the Nahe, not to be confused with Rüdesheim on the Rheingau. Rüdesheimer Rosengarten from the Nahe is a shipper's regional blend that is not infrequently seen here.

VILLAGE	IMPORTANT VINEYARDS
Schloss	
Böckelheim	Kupfergrube, Felsenberg, Königsberg
Niederhausen	Hermannshöhle, Rosenberg
Kreuznach	Narrenkappe, Kronenberg, Hinkelstein

Franconia

The wines of Franconia, shipped in the distinctive *Bocksbeutel,* are comparatively dry, less typically German in flavor, and characterized by a *Bodengeschmak,* or taste of the earth, that sets them apart from the more fragrant wines of the Rhine and Moselle. Frankenwein and Steinwein are often used as regional names for these wines, but the latter should properly be used only for the wines from the Stein vineyard in Würzburg. This vineyard, incidentally, is the single largest one in Germany—four hundred acres—and is entirely owned by the German Federal State. Here are some Franconia wines that might be found in shops with a fairly complete selection of German wines.

VILLAGE	IMPORTANT VINEYARDS
Würzburg	Stein, Innere Leiste, Schlossberg
Escherndorf	Lump, Kirchberg
Randersacker	Hohburg, Spielberg

The Wines of
Italy

FRANCE AND ITALY are by far the two biggest wine-producing countries in the world—together they account for half of all the wines made—and in most years Italy is ahead. Not only does Italy make almost two billion gallons of wine in abundant vintages, but it can claim title to being the most completely vinous nation of all, as vines are planted in just about every region of the country. Italian wines achieve great variety—red, white, and rosé; sweet and dry; still and sparkling—and not infrequently all of these characteristics can be found in the wines of a single district. Most of the Italian wines imported into this country are agreeable and uncomplicated, and they are comparatively inexpensive. Although even the best wines of Italy are not considered quite as fine as the very best of France and Germany, the quality of certain wines, notably from Tuscany and the Piedmont, is of a very high level. One problem facing the consumer is that the same familiar wine names apply to wines of variable quality, including the very best, whereas in France and Germany there are an abundance of individual vineyard names at the top level. A consumer can drink Chianti without being aware of the finest examples, or serve a Barolo without realizing that this wine will benefit as much from bottle age as will a château-bottled wine from Bordeaux. Another problem has been that the Italian government has only recently established wine laws as clearly defined and as strict as those in use in France and Germany.

Italy has been producing wine for almost three thousand years, and even twenty centuries ago wine was the daily

The Wine Regions of Italy

drink of the people. Italians have always taken wine for granted, and this casual attitude was reflected in the easygoing way in which much of Italy's vineyards were cultivated until fairly recently. It is still possible today to see the old *filare* system in various wine regions. A *filare*, or row, consists of small trees within whose branches a number of vines are intertwined. Plots of wheat, corn, or other crops separate the *filari*, which go back to a time when wine was only one of the products of a particular property. Nowadays, the *filari* are being uprooted and vineyards planted in a way that permits more careful tending and better use of the available land. Although old-fashioned wine making techniques are still used by many small growers throughout Italy, there has been a significant movement toward cooperative wine making and marketing organizations (*cantina sociale*), whose size permits them to employ modern methods and equipment.

The Italian's informal approach to wine making, combined with his traditionally individualistic attitude, made it difficult in the past to establish quality controls similar to those enforced in many other countries. In recent years, growers and shippers in several wine districts have banded together to form a *consorzio,* or committee, to establish certain minimum standards. This self-discipline varies in intensity from one *consorzio* to another, and in any case a local producer who chooses not to join can nevertheless continue to sell his wines on the market, but without the *consorzio* seal. In the past decade, the Italian government —spurred on by Italy's entry into the Common Market— has been taking a much more active role in establishing wine laws for the most important districts. These laws, which are in some ways more complete than those of the *appellation contrôlée* in France, have utilized the best self-regulations of the various *consorzio,* and the wines so affected now show the words *Denominazione di Origine Controllata* on their labels. The first laws were established in 1963 and went into effect in 1967. There are now about two hundred wines subject to these new regulations, many of which are rarely if ever seen in this country. Additions and further regulations will continue to appear as part of a long-term project to supervise the production of the most important wines, some of which are already controlled by the highest and strictest appellation, *Denominazione di Origine Controllata e Guarantita.*

Although these new wine laws are having an important effect on the quality and labeling of Italian wines, another factor which complicates any study of Italian wines is that their names do not follow any specific pattern. Some wines are known by the grape from which they are made, others by their village of origin, and a few are marketed with colorful fantasy names. Since the grapes used in Italy are not the classic varieties most familiar to consumers of French, German, and varietal California wines, it's not always easy to pick them out. Thus, Barbaresco is a village, Barbera a grape, Verdicchio another grape, Orvieto a town. To make matters even more confusing, the same wine may be red or white; sweet (*abboccato*) or dry (*secco*); still, lightly sparkling (*frizzante*), or fully sparkling (*spumante*).

These considerations might discourage an enthusiastic tourist about to make a wine tour of Italy, where several hundred agreeable wines are available from one end of the country to the other, and where a different and unfamiliar local wine might be offered with almost every meal. But for anyone who wants to enjoy Italian wines in this country, getting to know what is actually available is considerably easier. For one thing, only a dozen or fifteen wine names account for almost all the Italian wines sold here. For another, most of these wines bear the brand names of relatively few well-known Italian shippers. The attention to inner districts, individual vineyards, and the best vintages that is so important in buying the best of French and German wines, is replaced here by a few wines and a few brands. What's more, most of these wines sell for two to three dollars a bottle, the main exceptions being the expensive *Riserva* Chiantis and Barolos that sell for four to five dollars.

The traditional Italian wine bottle is the round, straw-covered flask, or *fiasco*. These colorful and decorative bottles convey much of the light-hearted and informal attitude with which Italian wines are best approached. As it is difficult to store these bottles properly on their sides, you can correctly assume that *fiaschi* are not meant to be put away for further aging. What's more, because they often have short, cheap corks, their bottle life is correspondingly short. Many shippers market the same range of wines both in *fiaschi* and in traditional bottles, and it is invariably the latter that contain the best wines. Because the straw that covers a *fiasco* must be woven by hand, the rising cost of labor has made *fiaschi* much more expensive than regular wine bottles, and Italian shippers would be delighted to do away with *fiaschi* if it were commercially possible. You should also note, when examining a label or making a purchase, that a normal wine bottle holds twenty-four ounces, but the *fiaschi* may vary from twenty-four to thirty-three ounces (a litre), and prices will vary accordingly. *Fiaschi* are also available in pints, half-gallons, and gallons.

Rather than approach Italian wines geographically, this guide begins with the best known and most easily available wines.

The region of Tuscany, with Florence as its capital, is the home of what may be the most famous red wine in the world: Chianti. Although Chianti is meant to come from a district stretching from north of Florence to south of Siena, the demand for this wine throughout the world had led many shippers to use any Tuscan red wine to make Chianti, and wines from elsewhere in Italy were not uncommonly used. As a result, what is technically a district name was used as a broad-based generic name for a dry red wine of variable quality. The new wine laws have now made this practice illegal, and their enforcement is having a continuing effect on improving the quality of the Chianti imported into this country.

Tuscany is a fairly extensive wine region which produces more table wine than does the United States. Only about a quarter of Tuscan wines are entitled to call themselves Chianti, and within the Chianti district is the delimited inner zone of Chianti Classico which accounts for about 15 percent of the wines made in Chianti. About forty years ago the top producers of this inner zone of Chianti formed a *consorzio* to establish and protect the geographic limits of Chianti Classico. Such wines bear neck labels depicting the *Gallo Nero*, a black cockerel on a gold background ringed by a red border. A Chianti Classico that has been aged in cask and bottle for at least two years may carry a seal that also incorporates an outer silver ring bearing the words Chianti Classico *Vecchio* (*vecchio* means old). The same *Gallo Nero* on which the silver ring is replaced by a gold ring with the words Chianti Classico *Riserva* can only be used for a wine that has been aged for at least three years. The last two variations on the basic *Gallo Nero* are not often seen here, and even the black cockerel seal itself is not so readily found on bottles of Chianti. Only a small proportion of the Chianti sold here is from the Chianti Classico zone. This seal should not be confused with the simple red seal bearing the legend *Italia INE,* which is an export sticker found on just about every bottle of Italian wine sold here.

Although the best wines are considered to come from the Chianti Classico zone, most of its two dozen or so producers make comparatively limited quantities of wine and only a few of them export their wines here with any regularity. A number of important producers are located outside the zone, and they make excellent wines as well. Their bottles are often entitled to bear the distinctive neck bands of other Chianti *consorzio,* among them the *putto,* displaying a blue cherub on a white ground. Seals other than the *Gallo Nero,* however, are not usually seen on bottles shipped to this country, as the shippers prefer to rely on their own reputations.

There are two aspects in the vinification of Chianti that set it apart from most other red wines. For one thing, about 20 percent of the vineyards are planted in white grapes which are crushed and vinified along with the red grapes, giving Chianti a certain lightness that it would not otherwise have. The other unusual aspect is the *governo alla toscano,* that takes place after the wine has been vinified in the usual way and transferred from the fermentation vats to large casks, or *cuves.* In November or December, bunches of grapes from the harvest that have been spread out in trays to lose some of their moisture are crushed and begin to ferment. This must—especially rich in sugar—is added to the casks of Chianti already made in the normal way, which now begin a slow second fermentation. The addition of this special must adds richness and suppleness to the very young wine, and helps to determine the character of Chianti as we know it. Since this second fermentation is very slow, taking place as it does during the winter, some of the resulting carbon dioxide gas can be retained in the wine if it is bottled within a few months of the vintage. The resulting Chianti, slightly *frizzante,* is quite popular in Italy, and Chianti ordered in *fiaschi* in the restaurants of Florence will often have this slightly sparkling quality. This is not generally true of the *fiaschi* shipped here, nor of any Chianti shipped in normal bottles.

It's certain that the quality of Chianti can vary greatly from one label to another. Unlike the equally popular wines of Beaujolais, which can be thin and coarse at worse, or fruity, full-flavored, and very refreshing at best, the possible range of Chianti is much greater. This is because a fine Chianti, unlike a Beaujolais, will have been aged in wood for two or three years or more, and will improve in bottle for another five. Whereas each vintage of the famous red wines of Bordeaux and Burgundy is kept in barrel approximately the same length of time before being bottled, the wines of Chianti (and of the Piedmont, Rioja, and parts of Portugal, for that matter) are judged only after they have begun to show their individual qualities. The best wines are then kept aside for additional aging in wood, so that it is not unusual for a firm to be bottling the wines of a recent light vintage while the bigger wines of a previous vintage are still maturing slowly in giant casks. These *Riservas,* as they are labeled, are wines of great style and depth of character, and they represent the finest wines that the region can produce. It is all the more unfortunate that so many Americans think of Chianti as a mediocre and somewhat bitter cheap wine whose decorative bottle can later be used as a candleholder. Actually, the best Chiantis are shipped in the traditional narrow-shouldered bottle used in Bordeaux.

There is also some dry white wine made in Tuscany, and most of the Chianti shippers market a white wine. It is now illegal to use the description Chianti Bianco, or white Chianti, so the wine will simply bear the shipper's brand name without a specific indication as to its origin.

Chianti producers whose wines are found here include Antinori, Brolio (which also markets a Chianti under the name Ricasoli), Frescobaldi, Nozzole, Ruffino, Serristori (under the names Machiavelli and San Andrea), and Straccali (which also owns Soderi and Suali). Two smaller producers whose wines are worth looking for are Vignamaggio and Pasolini Dal'Onda Borghese.

About eighty miles west of Venice, and just east of Lake Garda, is the historic city of Verona, whose local wines are almost as well known as is Chianti: Soave, Valpolicella, and Bardolino. The village of Soave (pronounced with three syllables) produces a pale, dry white wine with a great deal of charm if it is consumed young. It is not uncommon here to bottle white wines two or three years after the vintage, which gives them more character but less delicacy. Valpolicella and Bardolino are among the most enjoyable red wines of Italy—fresh, light-bodied wines with a characteristic dry aftertaste. Valpolicella is the sturdier of the two, Bardolino somewhat paler in color and lighter in body. The picturesque town of Bardolino is located along the eastern shore of Lake Garda, and many of its hillside vineyards are exposed to the extra sunshine reflected off the surface of the lake. Valpolicella is a valley north of Verona whose hillsides are covered with vines. The nearby valley of Valpantena produces red wines very similar to those of Valpolicella, but its name is not often seen on a wine label, since its wines can be marketed as Valpolicella.

An unusual red wine, Recioto, is made in limited quantities from selected bunches of grapes that are spread out on trays and left to dry until they have turned slightly raisiny. The resulting wine has considerably more depth of character than a Valpolicella, and may be matured in giant casks for five years or more. The wines that retain some of their natural sweetness are called Recioto Amabile and turned into sparkling red wines; the wines that ferment out dry are bottled as Recioto Amarone.

The major shippers of Veronese wines include Bolla, Bertani, and Folonari.

At the southwestern end of Lake Garda, in the Lombardy region, are vineyards producing some agreeable red wines and rosés. The rosés might be labeled Chiaretto del Garda, Chiarello, or Lake Garda Rosé, or they may bear colorful brand names without more detail about their origin. The nearby village of Lugana is known for its attractive white wines.

The best red wines of Italy—with the exception of the finest wines of Chianti—come from the Piedmont region, in the northwest corner of the country. Unlike the great majority of Italy's red wines, the Piedmontese wines need several years in bottle to develop their best qualities, and well-aged examples can be quite impressive with their distinctive character and depth of flavor.

What is generally considered the best of these wines is produced around the village of Barolo, just south of Alba, from the Nebbiolo grape. The new wine laws specify that Barolo must be aged for at least three years before being marketed, two of them in barrel, but it is not unusual to find five-year-old wines still aging in giant casks. Production of this wine is not extensive—the beautiful hillside vineyards around Barolo make about a third as much wine as is made in the Chianti Classico zone. The nearby village of Barbaresco also produces excellent wines from the Nebbiolo grape, in even smaller quantities. Gattinara, located about sixty miles north of Barolo and Barbaresco, is the third important Piedmont village producing excellent wines from the Nebbiolo grape, also in very limited quantities.

Apart from the wine of these three top villages, a great deal of red wine produced in the Piedmont is labeled with the name of the grape variety from which it is made. Barbera and Freisa are by far the most widely planted, and together they account for about as much red wine as is produced in all of Bordeaux. These delightful dry wines are known for their fruity bouquet and very agreeable style. Some examples may be *amabile*, slightly sweet, or *frizzante*, lightly sparkling. A wine labeled simply Nebbiolo is made from that grape, but in vineyards other than those of Barolo, Barbaresco, or Gattinara. Another red wine is produced in limited quantities from the Grignolino grape. Almost all of the table wines of the Piedmont are red, but some dry white wine is made from the Cortese grape, and so labeled. Among the best known firms in the Piedmont are Bersano, Borgogno, Fontanafredda, and Marchesi di Barolo (Opera Pia).

Turin, the capital of the Piedmont district, is also the center of the very important Italian Vermouth trade. The nearby village of Asti is famous for its aromatic sparkling wine, Asti Spumante, made from the Muscat grape: Vermouth and sparkling wines are described more fully in other chapters.

Three popular white wines are produced in three different districts in the center of Italy. To the east, near Ancona, on the Adriatic Sea, the Verdicchio grape produces a light-colored dry wine that is generally shipped in a distinctive amphora-shaped bottle. Verdicchio dei Castelli di Jesi, the highest appellation, comes from several towns in that specific district. A bottle labeled simply Verdicchio comes from vineyards nearby.

To the west, in the province of Umbria, the ancient walled city of Orvieto is known for its flavorful white wines. Orvieto, straw colored and having somewhat more character than most white wines, is available both as *secco* (dry) and *abboccato* (sweet). The wine comes in a distinctive squat, straw-covered flask, known as a *pulcinella,* and also in normal bottles.

Near Montefiascone is found the pleasant but undistinguished mellow white wine with the unusual name Est! Est!! Est!!! The name derives from a story about a German bishop who was journeying to Rome and instructed his servant to travel ahead and chalk *Est* (it is) on the side of those inns whose wines were worth a stop. The servant was so taken with the wines of Montefiascone that he wrote *Est! Est!! Est!!!* on the wall of a local inn. The bishop stopped and apparently concurred, as the legend states that he drank himself to death on the spot.

The white carafe wine of Rome comes from the *Castelli Romani,* a series of once fortified hill towns south of the city. The best known of these dry white wines comes from the village of Frascati.

Farther south, near Naples, are the vineyards producing Capri and Lacrima Christi. The enchanting Isle of Capri gives its name to a dry white wine most of which actually comes from the neighboring island of Ischia.

The slopes of Mount Vesuvius are planted in vines whose dry white wines are marketed under the evocative name Lacrima Christi or Tears of Christ. There is a little red wine available under this name, as well as a Lacrima Christi Spumante, a dry white sparkling wine.

In the north of Italy, in the Italian Tyrol, a number of wines are produced that are occasionally found in this country, although most of them are exported to Germany and Austria. Because this part of Italy once belonged to Austria, it is not surprising that Riesling and Traminer grapes are planted here, as well as Cabernet and Pinot Noir. It is claimed that the Traminer grape derives its name from the village of Termener (Tramin) in this district. Some of the best white wines of the region come from the town of

Terlaner (Terlano). These Tyrolean wines are cited because it can be quite a surprise to see wines in tapering German wine bottles with German-sounding names (most of the inhabitants speak German, rather than Italian) and then to note that the rest of the label as well as the country of origin is Italian.

In the northern province of Lombardy, very near the Swiss border, are the steeply terraced vineyards of the Valtellina Valley. The red wines, made primarily from the Nebbiolo grape, can be of excellent quality: the most famous Valtellina wines are Sassella, Grumello, and Inferno.

The village of Frecciarossa is unusual in that its vineyards are owned by a single family, so that this place-name has taken on the aspects of a brand. Red, white, and rosé wines are produced from these vineyards, of which the red is perhaps the best known.

Lambrusco, a rather special red wine, is made from the grape of that name in a district not far from Bologna, the capital of the Emilia-Romagna region. This wine retains a sparkling quality unusual for a dry red wine, although the wine is also made *amabile,* slightly sweet. Lambrusco is considered to be an excellent accompaniment to the rich local foods of Bologna, which is as important to the gastronomy of Italy as Lyon is to that of France. The Lambrusco shipped here tends to have only a hint of sparkle, and is characterized by a mellow, grapey flavor. This distinctive wine is the one best known from Emilia-Romagna, but several attractive dry wines are produced as well from individual grape varieties—notably the red Sangiovese and the white Trebbiano and Albana.

The most famous wine of Sicily is Marsala, described in the chapter on fortified wines. The island also produces a tremendous amount of robust and undistinguished wine that is traditionally used to add body and color to inexpensive wines from other Italian regions. Two wines from the western part of Sicily, near Palermo, are available here: Corvo and Segesta.

There is evidently a great variety of wine produced in Italy, and their names have a certain confusing quality. Perhaps more of them are listed here than one needs to know, and even so, these notes are limited to the kind of wine that is most often seen in this country under its particular label. Nevertheless, it is possible to find, for example, an Orvieto Rosé, or a Frascati Red.

In any event, most restaurant lists are limited to a Chianti and perhaps a Bardolino or Valpolicella for the reds, and a Soave or Verdicchio for the whites. Because these usually come from one of the major shippers, it's not difficult to find a particular Italian wine that you can depend on. If you expand your research to include, say, Orvieto, Frascati, and a white Tuscan wine plus one or two red wines from the Piedmont, you will soon have a pretty fair idea of the basic range of Italian wines. You can then experiment informally with the major brand names in each category to see which ones you find most to your taste. Remember that whenever a great deal of wine is sold under a few popular wine names, as is the case with Italian wines, the very cheapest wines will rarely have the characteristics that are associated with the grape or district name on the label.

Other European Wines

SPAIN

A TREMENDOUS AMOUNT OF WINE is made in Spain, which ranks third in production among European countries, after France and Italy. Although three-quarters of the fortified wines imported into the United States come from Spain, Sherry accounts for less than 3 percent of the wine made in that country and is not regularly seen outside of the district around Jerez. On the other hand, table wines in great variety are to be found throughout Spain where the per capita consumption of wine is nearly fifty times that of the United States. Spanish wines offer excellent value, especially the older red wines, and exports to this country, which increased dramatically in the past decade, have doubled in the past three years. In contrast to the Portuguese wines that are sold here—predominantly pleasant rosés—Spanish wine imports consist mostly of sound red wines.

The best wines of Spain, and the ones most often seen here, come from the Rioja district in northern Spain, not far from the French border. The vineyards extend for about eighty miles along the Ebro River, from Haro to Logroño and on to Alfaro. The district gets its name from a little river, the Rio Oja, that flows toward the Ebro near Haro. Wines have been made in this region for a very long time, and in fact the first attempt to guarantee the authenticity of these wines dates back to 1560. Today, Rioja is the most carefully controlled wine district in Spain, and its wines all bear a colorful back label depicting a map of the district and the words *garantia de origen*.

Although the wines of Rioja have long been known, the character of the wines produced was altered less than a hundred years ago, when phylloxera struck the vineyards of Bordeaux. A number of wine-making families moved across the Pyrenees to the nearby Rioja district and brought with them their vinification techniques. Now history has turned the tables, and as the Bordeaux growers have adopted more modern wine making methods, those of Rioja remain in many ways as they were in the nineteenth century. Basically, there is a longer vatting of grapes and must, so that the red wines are particularly rich in color and tannin, and the better wines are kept in barrel a comparatively long time: five or six years is not uncommon. As a result, the red wines often achieve great depth and maturity. Since even older Riojas are rarely over three dollars a bottle, and many sell for around two dollars, the best of these wines are among the very best values to be found today. Some white Riojas suffer from excessive aging in wood, but many producers are now adopting the modern

The Wine Regions of Spain and Portugal

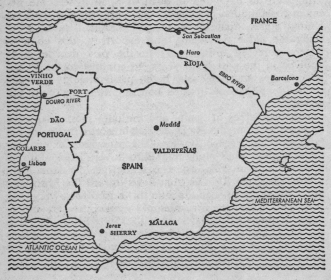

custom of bottling white wines within two years of the vintage to retain their fresh and lively taste.

Rioja is a comparatively large viticultural area, producing almost as much wine as is made, for example, in all of Burgundy. The vineyards are parceled out among thousands of farmers, most of whom also tend other crops. Consequently, the endless rows of vines typical of most wine regions are replaced here by plots of vines interspersed among wheat fields and olive groves. In recent years cooperative cellars have become increasingly important, and now account for over half of the annual production of Rioja.

Although a few of the major Rioja shippers own vineyards, just about all of them buy wine from farmers and cooperative cellars and blend them in their own cellars to produce a consistent house style. Most shippers also blend wines from the three principal inner districts of Rioja—Rioja Alta, Rioja Baja, and Rioja Alavesa—so the relative character of these wines is not of much concern to the consumer.

Because Rioja is a blended wine, and because there are no famous individual vineyards in Rioja, as in France and Germany, each shipper markets his wines under a number of brand names. This can be confusing to the consumer at first, because the names seen on Rioja labels, such as Viña Real, Viña Pomal, Monte Real, Banda Azul, and Brillante are proprietary names belonging to the individual shippers. Thus a firm's dry white wine will have one name, its mellow white wine another; its young red wine and its older *Reserva* wine will each be marketed with a different name. An analogy might be made, not with the vineyards and estates of other countries, nor with the generic labeling used in California and Australia, but with the Cognac shippers, who distinguish among their various grades by such proprietary names as Bras d'Or, Cordon Bleu, and Triomphe. Some cheaper Riojas are still labeled with generic place names such as Chablis and Burgundy, but this practice is less frequently encountered now.

A traditional practice in Rioja is for each shipper to market some wines in Bordeaux bottles, others in Burgundy bottles. As a general rule, red wines in Bordeaux bottles are somewhat lighter and more delicate, those in Burgundy bottles fuller and rounder, with a degree more alcohol. These distinctions are arbitrary at best, since the wines in both bottles have been made the same way from the same grapes grown in the same soil.

Vintages in Rioja do not have the same significance as in some other countries. Rioja is often a blend of several years, and a date on the label—sometimes preceded by the word *Cosecha,* or vintage—might only be meant to indicate the wine's relative standing among the grades marketed by that shipper. If a shipper has had success with the wine of a particular vintage, he may maintain that year on subsequent labels, using it as an indication of quality rather than as an accurate guide to age. Thus it's not impossible to find a young white wine with the unlikely legend *Reserva* 1930.

More important than a vintage date is the word *Reserva,* which indicates that the shipper has specially selected this wine, as it matured in his *bodega,* for further aging in cask and bottle. *Reservas* from the best shippers in Rioja represent the best wines that are made in this district, and they can be very good wines indeed. It's well worth experimenting with the Riojas available in various shops, as they are among the few imports which offer good wines for two dollars or less. The older red wines—the *Reservas*—are not much more expensive, and it is not unusual to find ten- or fifteen-year-old wines that compare favorably with older Bordeaux and Burgundies costing considerably more.

The well-known Rioja firms (and their popular brands) include Bodegas Bilbainas (Viña Pomal, Brillante, Cepa de Oro), Compania Vinicola del Norte de España, or CUNE (Viña Real, Imperial), Lopez de Herédia (Viña Tondonia), Marqués de Murrieta (Castillo Ygay), Marqués de Riscal, Federico Paternina (Banda Azul, Viña Vial), La Rioja Alta (Viña Ardanza), and Bodegas Santiago (Yago).

After Rioja, the district of La Mancha in central Spain is probably next in importance from the standpoint of quality. Red and white wines are made, of which the somewhat pale red is more easily found here. Within this district—the home of Don Quixote—the town of Valdepeñas produces the best wines of all.

Along the Mediterranean shore, north and south of Barcelona, are a number of districts producing interesting wines generally grouped together as Catalonian wines. The village of Alella produces a dry red wine and both sweet and dry white wines. Tarragona, south of Barcelona, was once famous for its inexpensive fortified red wine, known as Tarragona Port. Nowadays, production consists mostly of red, white, and rosé table wines. The village of Panadés, halfway between Barcelona and Tarragona, also produces agreeable wines, the best known here being those of the Torres firm.

There are a number of other red and white wines made in Spain that are of interest, such as Alicante and Ribeiro, but they are not often encountered here. As the better wines of France and California continue to rise in price, those of Spain will certainly become better known and even more widely distributed.

PORTUGAL

Historically, the most famous wine of Portugal is Port, but it actually accounts for less than 2 percent of this country's wine production and is not widely seen there. Table wine, on the other hand, is very much a part of the Portuguese way of life: about twice as much wine is produced in this very small country as in the United States, and the annual consumption is 125 bottles per person. Portuguese wines are becoming increasingly well-known here, and in the past ten years, as imported table wines have tripled in volume, those of Portugal have increased nearly twenty times.

The most popular wines of Portugal here are the many pleasant rosés, still and crackling, that are to be found in just about every store and restaurant. Often shipped in distinctive bottles and crocks, these agreeable wines have undoubtedly converted many people to the pleasures of wine drinking. The best-known brands are Mateus and Lancers.

Apart from rosé, however, Portugal produces a variety of inexpensive red and white wines that are becoming more widely distributed in this country. The best of these wines are now being made under the supervision of the Portuguese government, which has recently established wine laws similar in style and intent to the *appellation contrôlée* laws of France. At present, the six appellations of *vinhos de mesa,* or table wines, for which controls have been established are Vinho Verde, Dão, Colares, Bucelas, Carcavelos, and Moscatel de Setúbal. Bottles of each of these wines are entitled to bear a distinctive neck label as a guarantee of authenticity. The red Carcavelos and the white Moscatel de Setúbal are both sweet wines produced in very small quantities and rarely exported. Bucelas, infrequently seen here, is a golden, full-flavored, and somewhat dull dry white wine from a village of that name about fifteen miles north of Lisbon.

Vinho Verde, very popular in Portugal, is now becoming better known in this country. Its name literally means green wine, but only in the sense of new wine: it can be red or white. Vinho Verde is produced in the northwest of Portugal, in the Minho province, north of the Douro River. These light-bodied wines are comparatively low in alcohol, and when consumed locally they are noted for their refreshing acidity. Red Vinho Verde—one of the few red wines that is normally served chilled—has a rather harsh taste and is rarely exported. If Vinho Verde is bottled early, within a few months of the vintage, malolactic fermentation takes place in the bottle, giving these wines a slightly sparkling quality that adds to their charm. This natural *pétillance* is normally absent from Vinho Verde that is exported, and some of the white Vinho Verde that is available here is mellow rather than crisply acid, similar in taste to a mild white Bordeaux.

The Dão wines come from an extensive region in the central part of Portugal. The red wines—more easily found here than the mild, agreeable whites—are generous, full-flavored wines, often well aged and quite dependable.

About twenty miles from Lisbon, along the Atlantic coast, are the vineyards of Colares, which produce a very good long-lived red wine (and a little bit of undistinguished white wine). Although Colares is rarely seen here, the vineyards themselves are quite unusual and deserve mention. For one thing, the vines actually grow along the ground in sand dunes near the ocean, and planting new vines requires digging special reinforced trenches ten or twenty feet deep in the sand. For another thing, the Ramisco vines of Colares have never been attacked by phylloxera, so that this wine is one of the very few wines in Europe still being made from vines that have not been grafted onto native American rootstocks.

The vineyards along the Douro River are best known for Port, but they also produce table wines that are among the best to be found in Portugal. Because of the importance of Port in this district, it is unlikely that official appellation laws will be established for table wines from the Douro. Shippers are therefore marketing their red and white wines with proprietary brand names such as Evel, Planalta, Cambriz, Ermida, and Tuella, and some of these sound wines are now appearing in this country. The village of Pinhel, just south of the Douro, gives its name to a very agreeable red wine produced there.

Colheita, or vintage, *Reserva,* and *Garrafeira* are words sometimes found on Portuguese wine labels. One or another is used by a shipper when he wants to indicate that he has specially selected this wine for additional aging because of its superior quality.

SWITZERLAND

The little nation of Switzerland, with a population smaller than that of New York City, imports about three times as much wine as does the United States. Switzerland also produces a certain amount of wine, most of it white, and much of it agreeable enough: dry, crisp, refreshing, and uncomplicated.

Some wine is made in the Italian part of the country, but almost all of Switzerland's wines come from the French-speaking region known as La Suisse Romande. The cantons, or districts, that are best known for their wines are those of Neuchâtel, Vaud, and Valais. The most widely planted white wine grape is the Chasselas, known in the Valais as the Fendant.

Neuchâtel, the most familiar of Swiss wines, comes from vineyards along the northern shore of the Lake of Neuchâtel. This pleasant white wine sometimes has a *pétillant,* or sprightly quality, the result of malolactic fermentation, which produces a small amount of carbon dioxide gas often retained in the wine. Cortaillod, a village along the shore of Lake Neuchâtel, gives its name to an attractive red wine made from the Pinot Noir grape. A mellow rosé, Oeil de Perdrix, is also produced in this district.

The canton of Vaud, along the shore of the Lake of Geneva, is divided into two main wine districts: La Côte is the district west of the city of Lausanne, Lavaux is the district to the east. The wine villages of Dézalay and Saint-Saphorin, whose names appear on Swiss wine labels, are in Lavaux. Beyond Lavaux is the Chablais district, which encompasses the villages of Aigle and Yvorne. All of these wines are exported to this country, and they may be labeled with the name of the producing village, such as Saint-Saphorin or Yvorne, or with the village and district, as Dézalay de Lavaux or Aigle de Chablais.

The vineyards of the Valais lie along the Rhône River, on either side of the city of Sion. The wines of this district are labeled with the name of the grape from which they are made, sometimes in conjunction with the name of the district or its principal city—Fendant, Johannisberg, Fendant de Sion, Johannisberg du Valais, and so forth. A light red wine without much character, Dôle, is also made in the Valais from a combination of Pinot Noir and Gamay grapes.

AUSTRIA

Vienna may be famous for its coffee and its pastry, but wine is very much a part of the Austrian way of life: the per capita consumption of wine in this small country is over fifty bottles a year. Most of the wine made in Austria is white, and it bears a superficial resemblance to the wines of Germany. The same tall, sloping bottles are used, the Riesling and Sylvaner grapes are widely planted, and terms like Spätlese, Auslese and Cabinet are found on labels. The comparison is unfair to the pleasant white wines of Austria, however, as they generally lack the fragrance and charm of a Moselle and are less rich than a Rhine wine. Austrian wines are drier, with perhaps more character, and they often exhibit a pungent flavor reminiscent of Alsatian wines. Despite the common usage of the terms

Spätlese and Auslese, wines so labeled are almost consistently drier, without the complex sweetness of an Auslese from Germany.

The casual approach to wine that characterizes the Austrian enthusiast is most evident during the *Heurigen,* the new-wine festival that takes place every year soon after the vintage. Every grower who has wine to sell hangs a bough or wreath outside his house to alert passersby, and these refreshing wines are consumed on the premises in a yearly tradition that dates back almost two hundred years. A Viennese does not have far to travel, because good wines are made at the edge of Vienna itself, at Nussberg and Grinzing. Farther south are the villages of Gumpoldskirchen and Vöslau, and Gumpoldskirchner is probably the best known of Austrian wines. (As in Germany, the suffix *er* is added to the village or district name when it appears on a label.)

About forty miles west of Vienna, along the Danube, is the third major wine district of Austria, which includes the villages of Krems, Dürnstein, and Loiben.

Although Austrian wine labels are not as consistent as those of Germany, they are easy enough to read once you have the main wine villages in mind. Some wines are simply identified by their place of origin, such as Kremser or Nussberger. Other labels combine the place and the grape name: Gumpoldskirchner Riesling, Kremser Grüner Veltliner. Apart from the familiar German grape names there are a few found only on Austrian labels, such as Grüner Veltliner and Rotgipfler, and some Austrian wines are labeled only with the grape name, as in Alsace.

HUNGARY

Although Hungary is not one of Europe's biggest wine-producing countries, it has always maintained a special position among wine lovers as the home of the famous sweet wines of Tokay. At one time these luscious dessert wines were considered an essential part of any complete cellar, and the finest examples were served at royal banquets and state occasions. Tokay was assumed to possess special medicinal invigorating qualities that led doctors to prescribe it to dying patients, and bridegrooms would consume a glass to insure male heirs. No longer as popular as in the past, Tokay is nevertheless an interesting and unusual wine, enhanced by the legends that surround it.

The village of Tokay (spelled Tokaj locally) is situated in the northeast corner of the country, at the foothills of the Carpathian Mountains. A number of neighboring villages are permitted to market their wine as Tokay, and these hillside vineyards are planted, for the most part, with the Furmint grape. The volcanic soil of this district imparts a distinctive *terroir* to Tokay, a tang or undertaste that distinguishes it from the sweet dessert wines of Sauternes and the Auslese and Beerenauslese wines of Germany.

Tokay is made in a very special way. After the normal harvest, grapes are left on the vines to develop the same noble rot that affects the grapes in Sauternes and along the Rhine and Moselle. These shriveled grapes, with their much higher concentration of sugar, are known as *aszu*. The *aszu* grapes are specially picked and put into containers or butts, known as *puttonys*. A certain number of *puttonys* are then added to the normally ripe grapes, and the lot fermented together. The more containers of *aszu* berries that are added to a vat, the sweeter and richer the resulting wine will be, and consequently labels of Tokay Aszu indicate the number of *puttonys* that were added: five *puttonys* is the highest grade available in this country. Apparently, very limited quantities of Tokay were once made entirely from *aszu* berries, and this Tokay Essence has achieved legendary fame.

Apart from Tokay Aszu, there are also other wines made in the Tokay vineyards. Tokay Furmint is the normal wine of the district, and its label may carry the word *édes*, meaning sweet. Tokay Szamorodni is made from grapes harvested without special attention to the *aszu* berries among the vines (*szamorodni* means as it is grown). The wine may consequently be dry or sweet, depending on the proportion of shriveled berries that turn up in the vats, and this will be shown on its label.

Bottles of Tokay Aszu and Tokay Szamorodni contain only a pint, two-thirds of a normal wine bottle. The wines are so rich, however, that a glass with dessert is as much as most people will want to drink.

The other wines of Hungary come from several different districts scattered throughout the country. With few exceptions, Hungarian wines are labeled with a combination of the village of origin plus the grape variety used. One exception is the most famous red wine of Hungary, Egri Bikavér. The wine comes from vineyards around the village of Eger (just as German wine villages take on the possessive *er* when used on wine labels, so Hungarian towns add *i*), but Bikavér means Bull's Blood. This full-bodied dry red wine is made primarily from the Kadarka grape. Voros is a red wine grape whose name may appear by itself on a label.

A number of white wines are produced along the shore of Lake Balaton, which is the largest lake in central Europe, and referred to locally as the Hungarian Sea. Vines are grown along the slopes of Mount Badacsony, on the north shore of the lake, and two of the better-known wines are Badacsonyi Szürkebarát and Badacsonyi Kéknyelü. The latter, the drier of the two, is named after a grape variety, but Szürkebarát is a picturesque name meaning Gray Friar: the wine is made from the Pinot Gris. From the village of Debrö comes a sweetish wine with a peachlike bouquet, Debröi Hárslevelü.

With the exception of Tokay, Hungarian wines are moderately priced, and they are all shipped by Monimpex, the national export association.

GREECE

The vine may have appeared in Greece as early as 1500 B.C., and wine was certainly a common beverage in Homer's time, twenty-seven hundred years ago. Ancient Greek literature abounds in references to wine, and it's quite possible that these early Greek wines were of exceptional quality. Greece continues to produce a variety of wines today, and if they are not remarkable, many of them are nevertheless very sound and attractive wines.

To many people, Greek wine means Retsina, and in fact most Greek table wines are in this category. Retsina is a generic name applied to any wine that has been flavored, during fermentation, with a small but unmistakable amount of pine resin. Retsina has an unusual and pungent flavor that is described by those who do not like it as the taste of turpentine. Those who enjoy Retsina find it to be an excellent complement to the oily dishes that abound in Greek cuisine. Retsina is usually a white wine, but is also made as a red wine and a rosé, and is then labeled Kokinelli.

Apart from Retsina, there are a number of enjoyable red, white, and rosé table wines characterized by a distinctive and robust flavor that goes very well with rich foods. The problem for the consumer in buying Greek wines is that some names found on their labels refer to a place or to a grape variety, while many other names are the proprietary brand names of individual firms. Thus Roditis is a dry red wine or rosé marketed by several firms, while Hymettus is the name used by one firm for its white wine, and Demestica is used by another for both a white and red wine. The simplest solution in a store is to read a Greek wine label carefully. If you're in a restaurant, tell the waiter whether or not you want Retsina, and if not, tell him just how dry you want your wine to be. For example, the most famous red wine of Greece is Mavrodaphne, but it's a sweet dessert wine similar in style to Port, and not the best choice to accompany a meal.

YUGOSLAVIA

The wines of Yugoslavia are increasingly seen here, and these inexpensive red and white wines can be excellent value. Yugoslavia produces more table wine than does the United States, and its vineyards are located throughout the country. The best-known wines come from the northern province of Slovenia, part of which once belonged to Austria. It is therefore not surprising that extensive plantings now exist of Riesling, Traminer, and Sylvaner, as well as Merlot, Cabernet, and Pinot Noir for the reds. The cities of Lutomer and Maribor have often been seen on Yugoslavian wine labels, coupled with the grape from which the wine was made: Lutomer Riesling, Sylvaner de Maribor, and so forth. Recently, some of the biggest wineries have combined to market their wines in this country under the brand name Adriatica. These wines are labeled both with the name of the grape and with the village or district of origin, most of which are unfamiliar to consumers. Among the names to be seen on the Adriatica label are Sipon from Maribor, Rizling from Fruska-Gora, Cabernet from Istria, and Prokupac from Yovac. Sipon (pronounced *shee-pon*) and Prokupac (pronounced *pro-koo-pats*) are native Yugoslavian grape varieties.

RUSSIA

The vineyards of Russia have been considerably expanded in recent years as part of a government-sponsored program to increase the production both of table grapes and of wines. Russia now produces more than twice as much wine as does the United States, including a wide variety of sweet and dry table wines, fortified wines, and a considerable amount of sparkling wines.

The Wines of the
United States

CALIFORNIA

CALIFORNIA produces about three-quarters of all the wine consumed annually in this country, and its quality ranges from ordinary to outstanding. Although many consumers seem prepared to make—or to accept—general statements about the quality of California wines as compared to those of France, Germany, and other European countries, such comparisons are meaningless without specific information about the quality level of the wines being compared. Oddly enough, many wine drinkers who are knowledgeable enough to compare the wines of different villages in Burgundy or of neighboring vineyards in the Médoc district of Bordeaux, will casually group all California wines together, without distinguishing, say, among an inexpensive Mountain Burgundy, a distinctive Zinfandel, and a remarkable Cabernet Sauvignon produced in limited quantities by a small Napa Valley winery.

California produces a tremendous range of wines at different prices and of different styles, of which less than half are table wines. For example, there is a class of wines known as special natural wines—which includes mildly flavored wines with 20 percent alcohol, such as Thunderbird, and the newer fruit-flavored "pop" wines with less than 14 percent alcohol, such as Bali Hai—which nearly outsells all imported wines put together. Another more important class of wines is described as dessert wines and includes California Port, Sherry, Muscatel, Tokay, and other similar wines, many of them quite inexpensive, that are sweetened and fortified with brandy. These wines will

California: The North Coast Counties

be described briefly in the sections on Sherry and Port. Federal regulations prohibit the use of the word *fortified* on wine labels, and such wines are traditionally called dessert wines in this country. Although it is only very recently that table wines have begun to outsell dessert wines in the United States, this change in consumer preference indicates that more people are drinking wine at the dinner table than ever before.

California table wines can not be compared as a group to those of Europe. The wines that are imported even if not entirely limited to the cream of the crop, certainly include the very best examples of the very best vineyards of Europe. A tremendous amount of cheap and ordinary wine is made in France, Germany, Italy, Spain, and other wine-producing nations that we never even see here. What we do see all the time are our own inexpensive, dependable table wines of which California produces tens of millions of gallons annually. The very best of our own wines are just as difficult to find as it is for a Frenchman to find a Chambertin or for a German to locate a Steinberger Cabinet Auslese. The unflattering connotations of the word *domestic* have probably contributed a great deal to the condescending attitude that many Americans have about their own wines. The fact is, we have come a long way in a comparatively short time with regard to the quality of our wines, especially in light of the fact that many of the great European wine regions were established a thousand or two thousand years ago.

It was only two hundred years ago that the first vines were planted in southern California by Spanish missionaries. These Franciscan monks established additional missions throughout the state, and they planted vineyards as far up the coast as Sonoma, north of San Francisco. By the time that these clerical holdings were secularized by the Mexican government in the 1830s, European immigrants and farmers from the East had begun to set up commercial vineyards in California.

In the 1850s a Hungarian, Agoston Haraszthy, made a significant contribution to the wine industry by publishing the results of his experiments in grape growing and wine making. He later brought over about one hundred thousand cuttings from Europe, which greatly increased the number of grape varieties available to California wine-makers. In the last decade of the nineteenth century research conducted at the University of California indicated that certain grape varieties produced the best wines, and that these varieties flourished best in certain parts of the state. In effect, this was a scientific application of the process of trial and error that had been taking place for centuries in the vineyards of Europe and that is reflected in the *appellation contrôlée* laws of France, which limit the district from which specific wines can come and the grape varieties from which they can be made. These researches confirmed the growing awareness that the region north and south of San Francisco was best suited to the classic grape varieties that have traditionally produced the finest wines of Europe.

The gradual development of the California wine industry, which began on a commercial scale in the 1830s, owes a tremendous debt to the many Europeans who established wineries in the second half of the nineteenth century, including a Czech (Korbel), a Hungarian (Agoston Haraszthy at Buena Vista), a Finn (Gustave Niebaum at Inglenook), an Irishman (Concannon), a German (Wente), a Prussian (Charles Krug), and three Frenchmen (Paul Masson, Georges de Latour at Beaulieu Vineyard and Etienne Thée at Almadén). Then, less than a hundred years after it began, this industry was crippled by Prohibition. Small wineries went out of business, and only a few companies were able to survive by producing sacramental wines or by growing grapes to be used for home wine making, which was still legal. The better wine varieties were discontinued, and plantings were made of high-yield, thick-skinned grapes that could be shipped east without damage. To this day, about 60 percent of California wines are made from table and raisin grape varieties, which are crushed to produce dessert wines and inexpensive table wines.

After the repeal of Prohibition, commercial wine making started again almost from scratch, as there was a shortage of equipment, of tanks and barrels to store the wine, of land planted in anything but high-yield varieties, of skilled personnel, and of a public accustomed to drinking table wines. It's not unfair to say that wine making in California is, in a sense, less than forty years old.

California table wines can be divided into two general categories, according to the way they are marketed: *generic wines,* labeled with famous European place-names, and *varietal wines,* labeled with the name of the particular grape from which each wine is primarily made. Generic names have been used almost from the beginning of California wine making to suggest, in a general way, the kind of wine contained in the bottle. The most familiar generic names for red wines are Burgundy, Claret, and Chianti, and for white wines, Chablis, Sauterne (spelled without the final *s* in California), and Rhine Wine. These wines have only the vaguest resemblance to the wines that actually come from these specific places in Europe, and each producer will decide for himself which characteristics each of his generic wines will have. For example, Sauternes is a specific district near Bordeaux that produces sweet, luscious white wines made in a special way, yet much California Sauterne is dry, which makes the generic use of this name especially illogical. It is not unheard of for a winery to label the identical wine as Chablis and Sauterne.

Although this method of labeling wines obviously has its faults, it is nevertheless at the level of generic wines that excellent values are to be found among the many wines of California. If you experiment with the many bottles, half-gallon and gallon jugs on the market, you're bound to find some brands that are less expensive and more consistent in quality than many imported wines. You should note that some of these California jug wines—red, white, and rosé—are bottled with a small amount of sweetness in them, which may or may not be noticeable to your own palate.

In recent years many California wineries have been producing and marketing varietal wines from the best grape varieties used in the famous districts of Europe. These varietals include Cabernet Sauvignon, Pinot Noir, Chardonnay, Sauvignon Blanc, and so forth, and a given wine must contain a minimum of 51 percent of a particular varietal for its name to appear on the label. It is among these varietal labelings that the finest wines of California are to be found, but the best of them, which the experts are beginning to rate with the top wines of Europe, are still in very short supply. They flourish best in the cool North Coast counties around San Francisco Bay, and this area produces less than 10 percent of California's wine harvest. Even within this area, despite extensive new plantings of these top varietals, they still account for less than half of the crop. Because high-yield varieties grown elsewhere in California can produce four or five times as much wine per acre as these varietals and because the best grapes are also the most expensive, the finest varietal wines will never be cheap. Furthermore, an important factor in the quality of a varietal wine is the actual percentage of the named grape being used above the legal minimum of 51 percent. Since it is the specific character of each grape variety that distinguishes these wines and gives them their richness, depth of flavor, and quality, the extent to which a Cabernet Sauvignon or Chardonnay is diluted will have a tremendous effect on taste. It's especially interesting to compare the same varietal wine from several wineries, and because even the best California wines are marketed by brands rather than by individual vineyard names, this is the only way to determine your own preferences.

Red Wines

Cabernet Sauvignon, the classic grape of Bordeaux, produces the best red wines of California, and those from the best firms, with several years of bottle age, can be remarkable wines indeed. It is the well-aged examples of Cabernet Sauvignon that have most impressed the experts with their quality, and they are undoubtedly harder to find than a twenty-year-old bottle of Lafite-Rothschild or Haut-Brion. The *Ruby Cabernet,* a cross of the Cabernet Sauvignon and the Carignane, is an attempt to combine the quality of the former with the high productivity of the latter. Its agreeable wines are less distinguished than those of the Cabernet Sauvignon.

The excellent California wines made from the *Pinot Noir* grape are generally considered to be less complex, less fine and, in general, less similar to the Burgundy original than is the Cabernet Sauvignon to red Bordeaux. Nevertheless, a good Pinot Noir is a soft, round wine with a great deal of charm. The *Red Pinot* is the Pinot St. Georges, which is not a true Pinot at all, and its wines are considerably less interesting.

Zinfandel is one of the most widely planted of all the wine grapes in California and, while of European origin, has never been traced back to a specific European wine district. Its fresh and fruity wines are very agreeable and are usually excellent value.

The *Gamay* grape that is used to make Beaujolais in the southern Burgundy region of France is called simply Gamay or *Napa Gamay*. The *Gamay Beaujolais,* whose name is also found on wine labels, is not the true Gamay of the Beaujolais region (confusingly enough) but is now thought to be related to the Pinot Noir. The Gamay produces red and rosé wines with perhaps more charm and style than does the Gamay Beaujolais.

Other varietal wines include *Barbera* and *Grignolino,* from grapes widely planted in northern Italy.

White Wines

Although French wine laws still refer to the classic white Burgundy grape as the *Pinot Chardonnay,* recent studies suggest that the grape should properly be called the *Chardonnay,* and is not even a member of the Pinot family. This varietal produces the best of the California white wines, but they should not be directly compared to a Chassagne-Montrachet or Meursault from Burgundy. A California Chardonnay has a different style and somewhat less bouquet than its French counterpart, but it is nevertheless an excellent and distinctive wine.

Pinot Blanc, the second classic grape used in white Burgundies, is less widely planted here than the Chardonnay but is producing very good wines in California.

Johannisberg Riesling, which is the true Riesling planted in the best vineyards along the Rhine and Moselle, is also called the *White Riesling*. A Johannisberg Riesling has much of the flower and fruit for which this grape is noted, and the wine is often a bit mellow in taste. *Riesling* on a California wine label usually refers to a wine made from the Sylvaner and is less flowery but often delightful in its own way. The *Grey Riesling* is not a Riesling at all, but the Chaucé Gris, and often produces a wine of indifferent quality, despite its popularity. The *Emerald Riesling* is a cross of the true Riesling and the Muscadelle, and produces a mild, very agreeable wine.

Chenin Blanc, the grape used to make Loire wines such as Vouvray, produces very drinkable wines in California. The wine can be more or less dry, according to the style adopted by the individual wineries (as is the case with Vouvray, for that matter), and you should be prepared for this change of taste as you compare one brand to another. Chenin Blanc is also marketed as *White Pinot,* which is obviously misleading. The name probably originated as a corruption of the Chenin Blanc's local name along the Loire—Pineau de la Loire.

Sauvignon Blanc is the famous grape used in such different French wines as Graves and Pouilly-Fumé, and in California too its excellent wines can be either dry or sweet. There will usually be some indication on a label of the wine's relative mellowness.

Sémillon is the grape that gives Sauternes its special character when attacked by the noble rot. The dry climate of California prevents this beneficial fungus from forming naturally on grapes, and consequently Sémillon is often marketed as a dry wine. The label will indicate whether the wine is dry or sweet.

Two other dry white varietal wines are *Folle Blanche* and *Green Hungarian.*

Rosé Wines

Grenache Rosé is the best-known varietal rosé and is made from the same grape that predominates in the Tavel district of France. Other varietal rosés include *Gamay Rosé, Cabernet Rosé* and *Zinfandel Rosé.*

The region in which these grape varieties grow best is in the North Coast counties around San Francisco. Climatic comparisons were made between different wine districts within California and those of Europe, and it was found that California has temperature conditions that approximate those of such different regions as the Rhine and Moselle, Chablis, Bordeaux and Burgundy, northern Italy, Sicily and even Algeria in North Africa. In other words, certain parts of the state are best suited to high-yield grape varieties that can be blended to produce fortified dessert wines, others to ordinary table wines, and certain limited areas to the production of red and white table wines with the finesse and individual distinction of the best European wines. Just as the Chardonnay is not planted in Sicily or the Cabernet Sauvignon in the Rhône Valley, so there are appropriate areas for each kind of grape within California. Few people realize that there is such a range of climatic conditions in California, and even the best individual areas are not familiar to most consumers because their wines are marketed by brand names rather than California place-names.

There are several important grape-growing areas in California, but most of them do not produce the premium table wines with which we are presently concerned. The great Central Valley stretches for three hundred miles from Sacramento down through Lodi, Escalon, Modesto, and the length of the San Joaquin Valley beyond Bakersfield. This vast region, along with the smaller district between Los Angeles and San Diego, produces about 90 percent of the grapes used to make California wines, mostly from table and raisin varieties. The best land for varietal wines, however, lies near San Francisco, and includes the counties of Sonoma, Napa, Alaméda, Contra Costa, Santa Clara, Santa Cruz, Monterey, and San Benito.

Sonoma, which is north of San Francisco, was first planted in vines by the same Franciscan missionaries who introduced viticulture to southern California in 1769. Agoston Haraszthy established an extensive vineyard here in the 1850s—Buena Vista—which is still producing wines today. Other Sonoma wineries include Sebastiani and Korbel (known primarily for its California Champagne). Italian Swiss Colony, one of the two biggest California wineries, is located further north, in Asti. The biggest California winery, E. & J. Gallo, is in Modesto, in the San Joaquin Valley: it produces nearly one out of every three bottles of wine sold in this country.

The Napa Valley is generally considered to contain the finest soil in California for the classic grape varieties, especially Cabernet Sauvignon. A number of well-known wineries are located there: Beaulieu Vineyard (BV), Beringer/Los Hermanos, The Christian Brothers, Inglenook, Charles Krug, Louis Martini, and the new winery of Robert Mondavi, one of the most respected of all California winemakers. Smaller wineries, with limited production, include Chappellet, Freemark Abbey, Heitz Cellars, Mayacamas, Souverain, Spring Mountain, and Stony Hill. Hanns Kornell and Schramsberg produce California Champagne.

Alameda County and adjoining Contra Costa don't produce a great deal of wine, but the Livermore Valley in Alameda is well-known for its white wines. The leading producers in Livermore are Wente and Concannon. Weibel, an important producer of sparkling wines, is located in Mission San José.

Santa Clara is dominated by two important wine producers, Almadén and Paul Masson, and these wineries also own extensive vineyards (called ranches in California) farther south in Monterey and San Benito counties. The other wineries in this area include Mirassou and two with limited production, Ridge and Chalone.

One of the major problems that has faced those California wine-makers who are trying to produce the best varietal wines from the soil to which each variety is best suited, is that the nature of commercial distribution forces each winery to market a complete line of wines. The best vineyards in Europe produce a single wine, and even shippers who buy grapes, as in Champagne and Alsace, specialize in, at most, a very narrow range of wines. However, a California winery (some of which produce less wine than a Bordeaux vineyard or a German estate) is expected to market under its label varietal wines, generic wines, dessert wines such as port and sherry, and, if possible, sparkling wines as well. It's no wonder that an acre of California land may contain a number of varieties producing several different types of wine, while in a European wine district thousands of acres may be planted in one or two grape varieties. What this means is that each winery is not permitted to concentrate on making those wines that it can do best. One result has been the appearance in the past few years of small wineries that specialize in just a few varietal wines in limited quantities.

One sometimes hears it said that there are no bad vintages in California, along with the corollary statement that there are no variations in California vintages. The first claim is more or less true. The best European vintages are produced in most fine wine districts when the grapes ripen completely, which doesn't happen every year; in California, the climate is such that grapes will ripen properly and sound wine will be made almost every year. This doesn't mean, however, that all years are alike. The wine-makers themselves know that certain years have produced better Cabernet Sauvignon wines, others have produced outstanding Chardonnay, and that quality varies from county to county in the North Coast region.

The lack of attention given to California vintages, even for the best varietals, is based on several factors. For one thing, a California wine marketed with a vintage year must be made up 100 percent of the named year (which is stricter than the rules concerning vintages that prevail in France and Germany). Many wineries would prefer to maintain their flexibility by blending wines of different years to produce a consistent wine for the public rather than drawing the consumer's attention to factors that will complicate his wine selection. This attitude is certainly shared by wholesalers and retailers, for whom vintages necessarily create problems of inventory and continuity.

A further problem in the marketing of vintage California wines is that the best of these red wines naturally need the same bottle aging as do the best wines of Europe. The consumer is unwilling or unable to maintain the necessary cellar, as is the wholesaler and retailer. Until fairly recently, the wine-maker was even worse off, because if he decided to hold back his best wines until they had achieved a certain amount of age, they were subject to an annual California floor tax. In other words, he was paying taxes on the same wines year after year as long as he continued to store them in his own warehouse.

Despite these problems, there is an increasing tendency on the part of the California wineries to market wines that state the year of the vintage, and some of them are actually putting a part of their annual production aside, to be marketed only after these wines have achieved a certain maturity. This is more than the châteaux of Bordeaux or the growers of Burgundy are prepared to do.

When a label does not indicate the wine's vintage, it is sometimes possible to guess at it anyway. Glass manufacturers keep tabs on their production by means of a code blown into the bottom of the bottle, which often includes two digits indicating the year the bottle was made. Because wineries do not keep large quantities of glass on hand, you can assume the wine was bottled in that year, and then add two years for reds and a year for whites and rosés to calculate the year in which the wine was probably made. This can be helpful not so much to evaluate vintage years, but to determine the age of a wine, especially white wines and rosés, which should be consumed young. A final remark about California vintages: the best years bear no relation to those of Europe, six thousand miles away.

Apart from the year of the vintage and the varietal name, there are other specific indications on a California wine label that are useful to know. The geographical origin of a California wine can be stated on its label only if 75 percent or more of the grapes come from the named district, such as Napa, Sonoma, or Livermore. This is a useful guide to selecting some of the best varietals from the North Coast counties, but you should also realize that some of the most respected wine-makers have acreage in more than one district. They can therefore make excellent wines without being legally permitted to state anything more than the name of the grape and that of the winery.

The words *Produced and Bottled by* . . . (the named winery) indicate that at least 75 percent of the wine was produced by that winery. *Made and Bottled* . . . means that only 10 percent was produced by the winery itself, and *Bottled by* . . . indicates that all the wine may have been bought in bulk from other sources. An *estate-bottled* wine indicates, as it does in Bordeaux, Burgundy, or along the Rhine, that all of the wine was produced by the winery from grapes grown on its own property. This designation is rare because it is traditional for even the best wineries to buy grapes from other growers, especially as there is such a demand these days for Cabernet Sauvignon, Pinot Noir, and Chardonnay.

NEW YORK STATE

Although grape vines had to be brought into California, the earliest settlers in the eastern United States found a variety of native grapes growing wild all along the Atlantic Coast. Encouraged by this profusion of vines, a number of colonists imported cuttings of the European *vinifera* varieties during the seventeenth and eighteenth centuries, and tried to establish vineyards on the East Coast. Invariably these vines died, and we now know that this was a result of phylloxera, fungus, and temperature extremes to which *vinifera* vines were not resistant. In the early nineteenth century, successful experiments were carried out with existing native varieties, notably the Catawba, and native American wines began to be produced commercially in several states. These native grapes, made up for the most part of *vitis labrusca,* impart a pungent aroma and distinctive flavor to the wines made from them, and their taste may seem strange to those who are used to European or California wines. This flavor is described as foxy, and its tangy and grapey character is most typically exemplified by the Concord grape, which is also the one most widely planted in the East. The eastern vineyards, then, are planted for the most part with native American grapes that are not grown in any other wine district in the world, and their wines should be approached with this basic fact in mind.*

By far the biggest wine-producing area outside of California is in the Finger Lakes district of New York State, about three hundred miles northwest of New York City. The region gets its name from several elongated lakes that resemble an imprint made by the outspread fingers of a giant hand. Although the region is subject to great extremes of temperature, these lakes exert a moderating influence on the climate of the vineyards situated along their sloping shores. The first vines were planted in this district in 1829 in a clergyman's garden in Hammondsport, at the southern tip of Lake Keuka. A number of commercial wineries were

---

* Eastern wineries are permitted to add a sugar and water solution to their wines during fermentation to reduce the natural acidity of native grapes, and the finished wines may be blended with as much as 25 percent of California wine to diminish their *labrusca* character.

established in the decades that followed, but four wineries established in the second half of the nineteenth century now dominate production in the Finger Lakes district. Centered around Hammondsport are Taylor, Pleasant Valley (whose wines are marketed as Great Western), and Gold Seal. In Naples, at the tip of Lake Canandaigua, is the firm of Widmer. Although the Finger Lakes account for less than 10 percent of the table wines consumed in this country, New York State fortified wines and sparkling wines account for a considerably bigger share of the American market and are discussed in the appropriate chapters.

As in California, the least expensive New York State wines are marketed under generic place-names of European origin, such as Haut-Sauterne, Rhine Wine, Chablis, Claret, and Burgundy. Because *labrusca* grapes are used to make up these wines, they bear no resemblance whatsoever to their French and German counterparts or to California wines, all of which are made from *vinifera* grapes. It's not unfair to say that a wine drinker who has his first experience of a New York State Chablis or New York State Burgundy is in for something of a surprise. Nevertheless, people who enjoy the distinct flavor of certain table grapes find these wines very pleasing indeed, and their wide distribution in this country attests to their popularity.

A number of New York State wines are made from specific native grapes and are so labeled. These varietals include Delaware, Diamond, Niagara, Missouri Riesling (no relation to the Riesling of Germany), Vergennes, Isabella, and Catawba. These wines naturally have the typical *labrusca* taste, and their more precise labeling makes it easier for the consumer to choose among them. The widest range is marketed by Widmer.

In recent years there has been an important trend in the Finger Lakes vineyards toward French-American hybrids. These are crossings that combine the hardiness of the American vines and their resistance to disease and extremes of cold with the more delicate flavor of the *vinifera* grape. These hybrids, which are becoming increasingly important in the production of New York State wines, are named after the men who developed them and carry the serial number of the original seedling, such as Baco 1, Seibel 5279, Seyve-Villard 5276, and Ravat 6. These names and numbers lack sufficient glamour to be used by themselves as varietal wine names, but they are being adapted for use on wine labels. Thus Baco 1 is labeled as Baco Noir, Ravat 6 as Ravat Blanc, Aurora is the Seibel 5279, and Chelois is the Seibel 10878. These wines, in which the *labrusca* flavor is considerably diminished, are now being blended with native wines in some generics, and certain bottlings are now mostly composed of wines from French-American hybrids. In other words, one New York State Burgundy may be made up of wine from native vines, another firm's Red Wine may contain a proportion of hybrid wines, and a Sauterne might, for example, be made up entirely of a single hybrid. It's usually difficult to discover from a label what proportion of hybrid wines, if any, has been used, but a wine made primarily from hybrids will usually indicate this fact on its label. Great Western produces several wines that are made from French-American hybrids.

Some very significant work has been done by Dr. Konstantin Frank, who has demonstrated that *vinifera* grapes can be successfully grown in the climate of New York State. He first experimented grafting European vines on native American rootstocks with the encouragement of Charles Fournier of Gold Seal, and has recently established his own company—Vinifera Wine Cellars—to produce and market his *vinifera* wines. Pinot Chardonnay, Riesling, Gewürztraminer, Pinot Noir, and Gamay are some of the wines he has made, and the best of the white wines are exceptionally good. As a result of his pioneering work, other wineries, notably Gold Seal, have also been experimenting with *viniferas*. While the bulk of New York State table wines are still made from native grapes, the increasing use of hybrids and the beginnings of a *vinifera* production has caused many consumers to redefine their attitudes toward wines from this part of the country.

No description of American wines would be complete without mention of Philip Wagner's Boordy Vineyard, near Baltimore, Maryland. His pioneering work with French-American hybrids has probably been the major factor in the increased use of these varietals in other eastern vineyards. Boordy Vineyard produces small amounts of red, white, and rosé, almost all of which is consumed locally.

A new vineyard has recently been planted with hybrids in Westfield, New York, under Wagner's supervision, and these wines also carry the Boordy name.

Although Ohio was one of the earliest sources of American wines, its production today is considerably less than that of New York State. The Catawba grape is the most extensively planted by far, and the leading producer is Meier's Wine Cellars.

The Wines of
South America

CHILE

ALTHOUGH Chile is not the biggest wine-producing country in South America, the quality of its wines is considered to be the best of that continent. Some years ago, inexpensive Chilean wines of mediocre quality were widely distributed in this country, in the distinctive squat gourdlike bottle. It has taken some time for Chilean wines to overcome the first impression that was made on the American public, but the excellent quality of many of the wines now being exported have established them as very good value.

Chile extends for about three thousand miles along the west coast of South America, in a thin strip rarely more than a hundred miles wide, between the Pacific Ocean and the Andes Mountains. The country has a wide variety of terrains and climates, and the best grape-growing area for table wines is in the central valley of Chile, north and south of Santiago. Vines were first brought to Chile by Spanish missionaries in the sixteenth century, but wine making did not really get started on a commercial basis until the mid-nineteenth century. At that time French wine experts, many of them from Bordeaux, were brought over to Chile, as were a number of French grape varieties. To this day, there are extensive plantings of the classic Bordeaux vines, such as Cabernet Sauvignon, Merlot, Sauvignon Blanc, and Sémillon as well as Pinot Noir and Riesling. As a matter of fact, Chile has considerably more acreage devoted to these top varietals than does California.

Although Chile produces more table wine than the

United States (and has an annual consumption of over sixty bottles per person), almost all of it is sold in barrels or in large jugs, and very little is marketed in the familiar bottle sizes used by other countries. Exports, limited in the past, are now being increased under government supervision. The result has been an increase in the sales of Chilean wines here, and a significant improvement in the quality of the wines now available. Although generic names, such as Chilean Burgundy and Chilean Rhine Wine are still used, the better wines are labeled with the name of the grape variety used, and Cabernet, Pinot Noir, and Riesling wines can be excellent values. Two firms whose wines are often seen here are Concha y Toro and Undurraga.

ARGENTINA

Argentina has occasionally overtaken Spain as the third biggest wine-producing nation in the world, after France and Italy. Most of its production consists of low-priced table wine that is consumed within its borders: the average Argentinean drinks over one hundred bottles of wine a year. Recently, a number of Argentinean producers have begun to export their wines to this country, and these inexpensive wines can be found in a number of cities. The agreeable red wines seem to be more attractive than the whites and rosés.

Various Wines

AUSTRALIA

THERE ARE a number of interesting parallels to be drawn
between wine production in Australia and the United States.
Commercial wine making began at about the same time, in
the 1830s, and developed in a number of districts in both
countries rather than in a single area. Fortified wines were
produced in far greater quantities than table wines, and
only in the past few years has each country reversed that
trend. Moreover, the growth pattern has been the same:
fortified wines continue to be produced at a constant level,
while the production of table wines steadily increases, a
sure indication that more and more consumers are enjoying
wines with their meals.

James Busby, a Scottish schoolteacher, is often referred
to as the father of the Australian wine industry, and his
role seems to have been quite similar to that of Agoston
Haraszthy in California. Busby brought over a great number of cuttings in 1831, distributed them to a number of
growers in the Hunter River Valley, north of Sydney, and
also contributed a treatise on viticulture to aid new wine-
makers. Vineyards were soon established in different districts of Australia, in such places as the Barossa Valley
(north of Adelaide, and nearly eight hundred miles from
the Hunter River Valley), Coonawarra, Murray Valley,
Murrumbidgee Valley, Great Western, Tahbilk, and so
forth. Today Australia produces about as much table wine
as, say, the Beaujolais region of France.

Australia, halfway around the world, and almost as big
as the United States, is now sending some of its wines to
this country. They are generally well-made and are similar
in character and style to many of the wines from California.

As in California, most of the wines are made from several different grapes grown in a variety of soils—many firms own vineyards in several districts—and labeled with familiar place-names, such as Burgundy, Claret, Moselle, and Chablis. There is a trend toward using the district and grape name on a label (as a California winery might market a Napa Valley Zinfandel), but the problem, of course, is that the exotic Australian place-names are unfamiliar to consumers in other countries—which is precisely why winemakers rely on famous place-names to attract the wine drinker. Unfortunately, the use of famous place-names from France and Germany invariably invites comparisons, which can be unfair to Australian wines. For example, both a Burgundy and a Claret may be made from the same grape, known as the Red Hermitage, and similar to the Syrah used in the Rhône Valley of France. An Australian Moselle—surprisingly dry—may be made from the Riesling, but in Australia this refers to the Sémillon of France: the true Riesling of Germany is called the Rhine Riesling in Australia. What all this means to the consumer is simply that he must disregard the generic place-names used on the label, and rely on the skill and reputation of the individual shippers to provide well-made wines under their respective brands.

SOUTH AFRICA

Vines were first planted in South Africa by Dutch settlers in the middle of the seventeenth century, and its sizable production consists of table wines, brandy, and well-made fortified wines in the style of Sherry and Port. Most of its exports are shipped to England, its traditional customer, but South African table wines and fortified wines are starting to be seen in this country.

The Co-operative Wine Growers' Association, known as the K.W.V., controls wine production in South Africa, and presently accounts for almost all of the wines that are exported. The table wines available here are sound and well-made with certain similarities to the better wines of California: the reds are full-bodied, the whites agreeable but perhaps less distinctive. Paarl and Stellenbosch are two of the top wine districts, and these names can be found on labels.

ISRAEL

Although the wine production of Israel is relatively small by world standards (about half that of Switzerland, for example), Israeli wines are widely distributed in this country. Most of them are mellow red and white table wines and Sherry- and Port-type fortified wines, but some drier wines are now being marketed as well. Vines were growing in Palestine over three thousand years ago, but the modern wine industry of this country dates from the 1880s, when the Rothschilds sponsored the planting of vineyards. A co-operative society formed in the early years of this century now accounts for about three-quarters of Israeli wine production, and for almost all of its exports to this country, under the brand name Carmel.

ALGERIA

Algeria is an important producer of wines, although less so than before: several years ago Algeria made about three times as much wine as the United States, now the two countries are almost even. When Algeria obtained its independence from France in 1962, a great number of Frenchmen left the country, leaving the sizable wine industry without enough skilled personnel. At the same time, French farmers in the Midi, who produce enormous quantities of ordinary wine, began to protest to their government that imports of Algerian wine were hurting their sales. This has naturally affected Algeria's important export trade with France: the robust wines of Algeria have traditionally been blended with the lighter *vin ordinaire* of France to which they add color, body, and alcohol. Because Algeria is a Moslem nation, and Moslems are not permitted to consume alcoholic beverages, Algeria is in the paradoxical situation of having an important industry whose product can not be widely marketed within its own borders.

Champagne
and Sparkling Wines

CHAMPAGNE is the most festive of wines, and adds gaiety and distinction to any occasion at which it is served. Unfortunately, most of us drink Champagne only at crowded receptions, where we enjoy its convivial effect without the chance to really taste the wine as we would if it were served at the dinner table. It's a pity that Champagne is considered so special that it's reserved only for infrequent celebrations. Although good Champagne is never cheap (extra import duties are levied on sparkling wines), it is no more expensive than a good bottle of Bordeaux or Burgundy, and the appearance of a bottle of Champagne is unfailingly met with excitement and enthusiasm. Its exuberant effects have not always been appreciated, however, and Napoleon is reputed to have said, "When Champagne is drunk, proper distance is diminished. The wine was created to throw respect out the door."

Because Champagne is marketed almost entirely by brand names, it is not a difficult wine to buy. It's a wine, nevertheless, that is made in a fairly exacting way, and any visitor to one of the big Champagne houses in Reims, Ay, or Epernay invariably leaves with the impression that Champagne is not expensive considering the complex steps necessary to produce it.

There are any number of sparkling wines produced in France and throughout the world (these will be discussed separately), but true Champagne can be made only within the region of that name about ninety miles east of Paris. Although Champagne has been known as a wine for almost fifteen centuries, until the late seventeenth century the name described still, red wines. In the second half of the seventeenth century, the Benedictine monk Dom Pérignon, who was the cellar master at the Abbey of Hautvillers, noted that the white wines of Champagne developed a sparkle in the spring following the vintage. In effect, not all of the natural grape sugar had been transformed into alcohol at the time of the vintage, because early winters tended to halt fermentation before it ran its course. When warmer weather returned in the spring, the remaining traces of sugar began to referment, and the wines in barrel took on a natural effervescence. According to tradition, Dom Pérignon devised a cork to replace the ineffective pegs and rags that were then used to stopper bottles, and this enabled him, for the first time, to bottle the sparkling wines of Champagne in airtight containers. Dom Pérignon is credited with having invented Champagne, but what he probably did was devise a better way of retaining its natural sparkle so that the wine could be marketed. He also seems to have realized that a better sparkling wine was obtained if still wines from various Champagne vineyards were blended together before the second fermentation took place. He thus established the concept of a *cuvée*, or blend, which has enabled the Champagne shippers to maintain a consistent style year after year. It is this fact that makes Champagne unique, for unlike the best Bordeaux and Burgundies, which owe their distinction to the soil and exposure of a particular vineyard, Champagne is invariably a blended wine. More specifically, it is the one major wine whose sum, as a blend, is more distinctive than the sum of its parts: it is in blending that Champagne achieves its personality. One indication of this is the number of different Champagne firms in existence, each producing a slightly different Champagne by blending available wines in different (and secret) proportions.

The Champagne vineyards are generally divided into three sections: the Valley of the Marne, the Mountain of Reims, and the Côte des Blancs. About 80 percent of Champagne is planted in Pinot Noir grapes, the same variety that is used to make the great red Burgundies. The Chardonnay grape makes up the rest of the plantings, and is of course predominant in the Côte des Blancs. The major shipping houses own only about 20 percent of the vineyards, and most of the land is in the hands of thousands of small proprietors. At vintage time, these farmers sell their grapes to the shippers (who cannot rely on their own acreage alone to maintain their stocks of wine), at a price per kilo that is negotiated each year, just before the harvest. The established price of grapes is then multiplied by the official rating of the soil from which each particular load comes. There are a dozen villages whose vineyards are rated at 100 percent quality, including Ay, Cramant, and Avize. Others are rated on a sliding scale that goes down to 50 percent. About one-third of the wines produced in Champagne come from soil rated 90 percent or higher.

Because most of the grapes harvested are Pinot Noir and because the color of red wine comes from pigments on the inside of the skin that dissolve in fermenting must, it is essential that the harvested grapes be pressed and separated from their skins as quickly as possible. For this reason the shipping houses maintain huge presses at strategic locations throughout the vineyards, so that the journey from vine to press is kept to a minimum. It is to these pressing houses that the growers take their grapes, which are then loaded in lots of four thousand kilos, or nearly nine thousand pounds. The presses are wide and flat, rather than high, so that the grapes can be spread out and the juice can run out of the presses quickly. Two or three fast pressings produce the equivalent of ten barrels, each holding about fifty gallons. This is known as the *vin de cuvée* or first pressing (although actually more than one pressing is needed to produce this much wine). Three more barrels of wine are produced, called *tailles,* or tails, and this too can be made into Champagne, although this wine is naturally worth less. Finally a fourteenth barrel is squeezed out, known as the *rebêche,* and this wine can not be made into Champagne. The thirteenth barrel, incidentally, may be worth only 60 percent as much as a *vin de cuvée,* and there are some disreputable shippers who seek out the *tailles* to make a cheap Champagne. You can imagine that if these shippers further specify that their *tailles* must come from soil rated at, say 50 or 60 percent, there will be quite a difference between what they market and the wines of the leading Champagne houses.

The pressed juice is then transferred from the fields to the cellars of the shippers (or in some cases, to the cooperative cellars that exist in Champagne) and there the fermentation begins that will transform it into wine. When fermentation is complete, cold air is allowed to enter the cellars, so that the wine can rid itself of some of its tartrates, thus diminishing its natural acidity.

In January the tasting of the new wine begins, so that a *cuvée* can be made up for bottling. Each of the top shipping houses has, as always, obtained grapes from throughout Champagne to give itself flexibility in making up its usual blend. Tasting the new wines can take four or five weeks, and might take this form: first the wines of each pressing are tasted (those ten barrels that make up a first pressing) and compared to other lots from the same district. Then the wines of different Champagne districts are compared, and their respective qualities noted. One village produces wine known for its bouquet, another for its body, a third for its delicacy and finesse, and so on. Finally, wines on hand from previous vintages are tasted to determine in what proportion they should be used. Remember that a nonvintage Champagne (and this accounts for most of the total) is made up of wines of more than one harvest. This means that older wines have been kept in reserve and must now be used. Certain years produce rather thin wines, others big, rich wines that are too full-blown to be used by themselves. It is this complicated and delicate blending process that is the key to determining and maintaining a house style, upon which the reputation of each firm rests.

When a vintage is considered especially good, a vintage year is declared, the wines are made predominantly from grapes harvested in that year, and the bottles display the vintage year on their labels. Paradoxically, a Champagne made entirely from the wines of a single harvest tend to be less typical of a shipper's style, since older wines can not be used to balance the *cuvée*. For instance, 1959 was too publicized to be passed up as a vintage year, but many firms had trouble making a wine with the finesse characteristic of Champagne, since 1959 produced such big, full-bodied wines. The subsequent nonvintage, made from 1959s and the thinner 1960 wines, was privately considered more successful.

Once the *cuvée* has been made up, the wines are bottled. A little bit of sugar syrup—*liqueur de tirage*—is added to the wine, along with yeast, to provide the elements necessary for a secondary fermentation. The bottle is firmly stoppered with a temporary cork and is placed on its side. The sugar will now be transformed into alcohol and carbon dioxide gas, and because the gas is imprisoned in the bottle, it must combine with the wine. This chemical combination is the reason why bubbles last so long in Champagne, compared to carbonated wines. The artificially induced secondary fermentation in the bottle, which is the essence of the Champagne process *(méthode champenoise)*, takes a few months. Then the bottles, now filled with sparkling wine, are left to mature for a minimum of a year, and often for two or three years.

It was 150 years after Dom Pérignon first conducted his experiments that the key step of bottle fermentation could be adequately controlled. A French chemist devised a way to measure any residual sugar left in the still wine after blending, as well as a method for calculating how much additional sugar had to be added to the wine to produce the desired amount of gas pressure in the bottle. Until then, Champagne making was a fairly hazardous undertaking, as the pressure resulting from a secondary fermentation could not be controlled, and the bottles of the day were not uniform. It was not unusual for half a cellar to be destroyed by a series of bottle explosions. Today such breakage has been reduced to 1 percent, but Champagne production is so immense that a big firm might still lose ten thousand bottles a year in this way.

The maturing bottles rest in piles that stretch out literally for miles below the ground. The extraordinary underground cellars of Champagne are carved out of the chalky subsoil of the region, and enable the Champagne producers to maintain their enormous stocks of bottles at a very constant temperature. There are about two hundred miles of underground cellars below the vineyards of Champagne, and some firms maintain little railroads to transport the bottles from one part of the cellar to another.

A by-product of the second fermentation is a cloudy deposit that makes the bottle essentially unsalable. A series of complicated steps now takes place whose sole purpose is to rid the bottle of this deposit without losing the imprisoned gas bubbles. The bottles are put into *pupitres,*

A-shaped wooden boards with holes in which each bottle can be separately manipulated. A *remueur,* the most highly paid worker in a Champagne house, now takes each bottle, which is at a slight downward slant, and gives it a little twist to dislodge the sediment, while at the same time tipping the bottle over slightly to lower the corked end. This delicate process goes on every day for several weeks, and ends with each bottle resting vertically upside down— *sur pointe*—with all of its sediment lying against the cork.

The *dégorgement,* or disgorging process, is most easily effected by dipping the necks of the bottles in a cold brine solution, which freezes the sediment to the temporary cork. The *dégorgeur* twists the cork with a pair of special pliers, and it flies out with the sediment and a bit of wine. The *dégorgeur* sniffs the open bottle to see if the wine is corky, and then places it on a conveyor so that the final cork, the one we see, can be quickly inserted under tremendous pressure. A common arrangement that keeps the *dégorgeur* on his mettle is to give him a bonus for each corky bottle that he detects, but to fine him if it turns out to have been faultless.

Just before the final cork is inserted, some syrup is added to the wine, along with as much Champagne as is needed to fill up the bottle again. This *liqueur d'expédition* is what determines the relative dryness of a Champagne. The driest of all Champagne is *Brut,* which receives the least amount of syrup. *Extra Dry* or *Extra Sec,* the next driest style, does not taste as crisp as a *Brut. Dry* or *Sec* is in fact, not so dry, and *Demi-Sec* is the sweetest Champagne usually found here.

A Champagne shipper will occasionally say that Americans like to see the word *Brut* on the label, but actually prefer the taste of *Extra Dry,* and that may be true. Fashions change, and a hundred years ago English wine merchants unsuccessfully beseeched their French suppliers to send over some dry Champagnes to counteract the prevailing taste for very sweet wines. It was only in the 1870s that dry Champagnes established their present popularity, although certain markets—South American and Russia, for example—still demand fairly sweet Champagnes. Because the relative sweetness of a Champagne is determined only when the final cork is inserted, it is not difficult for any shipper to make up a Champagne that will conform to his customer's demands.

One aspect of *Brut* Champagne that deserves mention is that the less sweetening added, the better the wine has to be, as its quality can not be masked. Conversely, a *Brut* does not taste its best when served with a very sweet dessert—the sugar in the food seems to turn the wine slightly bitter by contrast—and it is the custom in Reims and Epernay to serve an *Extra Dry* with dessert.

It's worth noting here that the bottle-fermentation method described is used only for half-bottles, bottles, and magnums (which hold two bottles). Other sizes are produced by decanting bottles of Champagne into six-ounce splits and into larger sizes such as the jeroboam (four bottles) and methuselah (eight bottles). Evidently, splits have the greatest chance of going flat, and are in any case poor value, ounce for ounce, compared to a half bottle or bottle.

The difference between a nonvintage and a vintage Champagne has been explained. A vintage Champagne of a good house costs about $1.50 a bottle more than the nonvintage, and I think most shippers would be happy to base their reputation—and your enjoyment—on their nonvintage.

Some Champagnes are marketed as *Blanc de Blancs*, which is a specific indication that the wine has been made only from white grapes—the Chardonnay. A *Blanc de Blancs* tends to be lighter and more delicate, and there are many who prize its particular elegance. Note that this phrase has a very particular meaning in Champagne, where most of the (white) wines are made from black grapes. But when the phrase is used on wine labels from other districts, it can not have any meaning, because other white wines are always made from white wine grapes as a matter of course.

Some shippers market a *crémant,* which is a wine that does not have the full sparkle of a Champagne, but rather a more delicate *pétillance. Crémant* should not be confused with Cramant, which is a village in the Côte des Blancs whose wines are occasionally marketed under its own name.

The Champagne district also produces a small quantity of nonsparkling white wines. Of course, all Champagne begins as a still wine, but these go to market as such.

Technically called a *Vin Nature de la Champagne*, they are becoming increasingly hard to find in France, because the demand for wine with which to make Champagne is increasing with every vintage. It is almost impossible to find still Champagne outside France because the government apparently thinks the wine is too delicate to be successfully exported, and makes it illegal to do so. Sometimes a Champagne house will ship a few cases to a favored customer and label the wine "Chablis."

Finally, a few words about serving Champagne. There are few sounds that fill us with as much pleasant anticipation as the loud pop of a Champagne cork, but this is usually accompanied by a wasteful explosion of foam and wine. If you ever have occasion to open more than one bottle of Champagne at a time, it's worth noting the simplest and most effective means of doing it. The usual method is to grab the neck and start tugging at the cork. This means that the heat of your hand is applied to the narrowest part of the bottle, which is under greatest pressure, and the tugging only serves to increase that enormous pressure. Instead, put a napkin or handkerchief between your hand and the bottle (this is also a safety measure, if a bottle should ever crack), and first remove the foil and then the wiring. The bottle should be pointed away from yourself or anyone else, because once the wire is loosened, the cork may explode out. Be especially careful of a bottle that has just been carried from somewhere else, by yourself or a guest, as this agitation will have increased the normal pressure. Hold the cork firmly in your other hand and twist the bottle away from the cork. The cork should come out easily, but if it doesn't, you'll have to carefully push the cork away from the bottle with your thumb. As the cork comes out, the bottle should be at a 45° angle, so that a larger surface of wine is exposed to the atmosphere, and there is consequently less chance of pressure building up at the neck and wine spilling out of the bottle. This procedure may be a bit too deliberate for celebrating a sports victory in a locker room, but you'll find it's easy enough in your home.

The so-called champagne glasses so often used at receptions—wide, shallow, sherbet-type—are in fact the worst of all. Their flat, wide bottom surface dissipates the bubbles very quickly, and they are clumsy and unwieldy in the first place. The flute, a curved glass tapering to a point at the base, or the traditional elongated V, are both better glasses, as is the all-purpose tulip-shaped wine glass. If the bubbles rise from a single point at the base of the glass, they will last longer and present a more attractive appearance.

Here is an alphabetical list of Champagnes that can readily be found in the United States. There are, of course, other shippers doing business here, but these firms account for almost all Champagne sales in this country: the three firms of Piper-Heidsieck, Mumm, and Moët et Chandon account for two-thirds of all the bottles sold.

Ayala	Moët et Chandon
Bollinger	Mumm
Veuve Clicquot-Ponsardin	Perrier-Jouët
Heidsieck Monopole	Piper-Heidsieck
Charles Heidsieck	Pol Roger
Krug	Pommery et Greno
Lanson	Roederer
Laurent Perrier	Ruinart
Mercier	Taittinger

Although the Champagne region of France produces, by general accord, sparkling wines with the greatest style and finesse, Champagne accounts for less than half of all the sparkling wines imported into the United States, and for less than 10 percent of the sparkling wines consumed here annually.

In France, all sparkling wines not produced in Champagne are called *mousseux,* no matter how they are made. The best *mousseux* are made by the *méthode champenoise,* that is, by individual bottle fermentation. Among the best known bottle-fermented *mousseux* of France are Sparkling Vouvray, Sparkling Saumur, and Sparkling Seyssel. Red Sparkling Burgundy is also popular in this country, although it is not easily found in France. It naturally bears no relation to the fine wines of the Côte de Nuits and the Côte de Beaune, as only the least attractive wines in all of Burgundy are transformed into this sweet, sparkling red wine.

A second method in common usage throughout the world for the production of sparkling wines is the Bulk Process of tank fermentation, also known as *cuve close*. The second fermentation of the base wine takes place in large sealed tanks, rather than in individual bottles. The resulting sparkling wine is then drawn off under pressure and bottled. This method, also called the Charmat Process after the Frenchman who first developed it about sixty years ago, is obviously much quicker and cheaper than bottle fermentation. The agreeable sparkling wines produced by the Bulk Process will never achieve the distinction of Champagne or even of bottle-fermented wines from the same region.

The sparkling wines of Italy—dry or sweet, white or red—are labeled *spumante*, and the most famous comes from the village of Asti. Asti Spumante is made from the aromatic Muscat grape, and it has a distinctively sweet, grapey flavor that many people find delicious with fruit and dessert.

Sekt is the generic name for German sparkling wines, which are produced in tremendous quantities. Historically, the thin, acid German wines of poor years were used as the base for Sekt, but demand has become so great that quite a bit of wine imported from neighboring countries is now used as well. Today, more sparkling wine is made in Germany than in Champagne. Sekt is an agreeable wine characterized more by a fruity taste and a slight sweetness than by delicacy.

About 85 percent of all sparkling wines sold in this country are made in California and New York State. The word Champagne is permitted to be used to describe American sparkling wines, along with a clear indication of its origin: California, New York State, American. A large proportion of American sparkling wines are made by the Bulk or Charmat Process, and this fact must be shown on the label. Whatever the method used—Bulk Process or bottle fermentation—the quality of the finished wine will depend on the quality of the base wine used. Often it is simply a neutral white wine that can be transformed into an agreeable, if undistinguished, sparkling wine. A number of California wineries are making an effort to use more of the Chardonnay and Pinot Blanc grapes that are used in the Champagne district, with excellent results. Among the best known of the California Champagne houses are Almadén, Korbel, Hanns Kornell, and Paul Masson; other large producers include Christian Brothers and Weibel.

New York State Champagne is very popular throughout the country, and far outsells French Champagne. The native grapes, notably Delaware and Catawba, that give New York State wines a special grapey flavor are able to produce a very agreeable sparkling wine with a flavor of its own. The major producers of New York State Champagne are Taylor, Great Western, and Gold Seal.

The white and pink sparkling wines produced in America are usually called Champagne, the red wines are labeled Sparkling Burgundy. Cold Duck, a sparkling wine that has recently become quite popular and which is now being marketed by most firms, is a blend made up of Champagne and Sparkling Burgundy.

No consideration of sparkling wines would be complete without mention of the rosés from Portugal. These wines, usually sold in attractive crocks, are referred to as crackling and are, in fact, carbonated wines. Their popularity increased so dramatically that in some recent years Portugal exported more sparkling wine to the United States than did France. The best-known brand is Mateus Spiral.

Fortified Wines

FORTIFIED WINES are those to which a certain amount of grape brandy has been added to bring the total alcoholic content up to 17 to 21 percent. Wine producers in this country refer to such wines as dessert wines. Sherry and Port are the most famous examples of fortified wines, and Madeira, Marsala, and Málaga are also fairly well-known. Vermouth is a fortified wine that has also been flavored with a variety of herbs, and aperitif wines are made in a similar way.

It is common to divide fortified wines into two classes—the dry wines that are best served before meals and the sweet ones, which traditionally make their appearance after dinner. In practice, however, this division has too many exceptions. Some people like a sweet Sherry before a meal, the French themselves often drink a sweet Port before sitting down to dinner, and both sweet and dry Vermouth are often served along with cocktails.

SHERRY

Sherry is perhaps the most versatile of all wines: it can be bone dry, mellow, or richly sweet; it can be served before or after a meal, or at almost any time of the day. The name Sherry derives from the town of Jerez de la Frontera, in the southwest corner of Spain, and it may be well to note that true Sherry can come only from that small district, just as Champagne comes from the district near Reims, and Cognac from vineyards surrounding that town in southwest France. Until the thirteenth century this part of Spain was under Moorish domination and Jerez was considered the frontier (*frontera*) between the Moors and the Christians.

Jerez, which is the center of the Sherry trade, forms a triangle with the towns of Puerta de Santa Maria and Sanlúcar de Barrameda, and within this triangle are found the best grape-growing districts for the making of Sherry. The best soil, *albariza,* is made up of white chalk, and the district is planted predominantly with the Palomino grape. A certain amount of Pedro Ximinez is also planted, and the P.X., as it is called, is vinified in a special way to make very sweet wines used in the final blending of Sherries. Jerez is one of the few areas in the world where grapes are to some extent still crushed under foot in *lagares,* or wooden troughs (the workers actually wear specially designed hob-nailed boots) and vintage time is celebrated with one of the most famous of all wine festivals.

The juice is fermented into a completely dry wine, with no residual sugar, and is then stored in barrels in the *bodegas*—high-ceilinged warehouses—of the various firms. One of the most interesting aspects of Sherry is that wines from the same district, even from the same vineyard, will not develop along the same lines as they age in barrel. Not only will adjoining barrels develop wines of widely varying quality, but some wines will develop a *flor,* or flower, and some will not. The *flor* is a film of yeast cells that covers the wine's surface (the barrels are not completely filled so as to let the *flor* develop), and its effect is to give the wine a unique flavor. Wines attacked by *flor* will develop into Finos, the others will be set aside as Olorosos. At this point, when the direction of each barrel has been determined, a little grape brandy is added to the wine to help stabilize it. Additional brandy may also be added when the wines are prepared for shipment, to bring the total up to about 20 percent.

As the Finos and Olorosos continue to age, they are earmarked for the different *soleras:* it is the *solera* system that is at the heart of the making of Sherry, and is unique to its wines. In theoretical terms, a *solera* might consist of three rows of barrels, all containing wines similar in style, with the oldest wines at the bottom. When some of the wine in the bottom row is drawn off to be bottled and shipped, the loss is made up from wines in the second tier, which are in turn replaced with wines from the top row. The top barrels are replenished with wines from a *criadera,* or nursery, of still younger wines. Because no barrel is ever emptied of more than half its contents, older wines can continually impart their flavor and character to younger wines. The *solera* system enables the shipping firms of Jerez to maintain a continuity of style for each of their Sherries, year after year. In practice, of course, there may be half a dozen or more levels to a *solera,* and its wines are rarely kept one on top of another in sequence. Also, to make up a particular style of Sherry, a shipper will often combine wines from several *soleras,* so that the blend consists of wines of different ages and of different styles. Because all Sherries are made by the *solera* system, Sherry does not carry a vintage nor is it identified by the name of an individual vineyard.

Sherries are grouped into four main categories. A Manzanilla is a Fino that has been matured in the seacoast village of Sanlúcar de Barrameda. The salt air seems to give these wines a special tang, and a Manzanilla is the driest of all Sherries. A Fino is a dry sherry, but the word does not always appear on a shipper's label—colorful brand names abound. An Amontillado is an aged Fino that has developed a certain depth of character and is, in a way, the most Sherry-like of all Sherries. Once again, the word does not always appear on Sherry labels, and some Amontillados are less dry than others, and exhibit less character. The name, incidentally, is derived from Montilla, a village a hundred miles away whose excellent, unfortified wines are similar to Sherry.

Although an Oloroso is completely dry as it ages in its *solera,* its bigger body and bigger character lends itself to transformation into a Cream Sherry by the addition of sweetening during the final stages of blending. It's evident, then, that there are not only several basic styles of Sherry, but also that each shipper can make up a Fino, Amontillado, or Cream Sherry in his own way. The dry Sherries are usually served chilled, and many people like to drink Sherry "on the rocks." An open bottle of Sherry will last much longer than will a table wine, because of its higher alcoholic content, but a good Sherry, especially a dry one, will eventually start to lose its flavor.

Some of the best-known Sherry houses, along with their leading brand names, are: Pedro Domecq (La Ina); Duff

Gordon; Gonzalez, Byass (Tio Pepe); Harveys of Bristol (Bristol Cream); and Williams & Humbert (Dry Sack).

Sherry is made in California and New York State, and in fact California makes considerably more Sherry than Spain. Most of the American Sherries are made by the Madeira process, which involves baking the wines in hot rooms to age them artificially. Consequently, the drier Sherries are often less successful than the Cream Sherries whose taste can be more easily masked. New York States wineries have been successful in making very agreeable medium-dry and sweet Sherries that are comparatively free of the special taste of wines made from native American grapes. Some American wineries age their Sherries in small barrels instead of using the baking process, and there is even a small amount of Sherry now being made according to the traditional *flor* method, using cultivated yeast. Although Sherries produced in the United States generally lack the distinctive nutty quality typical of Spanish Sherry, many of them are soundly made and the best of them are a very good value.

PORT

Port is a sweet, red, fortified wine made along a delimited section of the Douro River in northern Portugal. (White Port has also been made for a hundred years, but it's not the same thing.) Port takes its name from the town of Oporto, at the mouth of the Douro, although the offices and warehouses of the famous Port shippers are located across the river in Vila Nova de Gaia. Port has always been very popular with the English, and was in fact specifically developed for the British market, but it has never really caught on in this country. It may be that certain cheap imitations produced by American wineries have diverted consumers from knowing how good authentic Port can be, or it may be that our drinking habits don't lend themselves to the appreciation of a sweet red wine that can be enjoyed anytime during the day, as well as after a meal. In an effort to resolve some of the confusion that exists about Port, the Portuguese government recently took the unusual step of officially changing the name Port to Porto, to distinguish the wine made along the Douro from wines labeled Port produced in America, South Africa, Australia, and elsewhere. As it happens, a certain amount of excellent Port sold in the United States is first shipped in bulk to England, and English-bottled Port is not bound by the new ruling.

Until the early eighteenth century the red wines of the Douro were known as unexceptional table wines. Political considerations then made it cheaper for the English to import wines from Portugal than from France, and as more Portuguese wines were exported to England, some shippers began to add brandy to the wines to fortify them for the long voyage. Gradually Port as we know it today evolved, and English novels of the nineteenth century abound with references to the pleasures of drinking Port after dinner, when the ladies have retired to another room. Today Port continues to be popular in England, but astonishingly enough, France now imports twice as much of this wine as does England. The French drink Port before the meal, as an aperitif.

Port is made in a very special way. The grapes are crushed; the juice begins to ferment; and while fermentation is still going on, brandy is added to the incompletely fermented wine. This sudden dose of alcohol stops the fermentation completely, and the resulting fortified wine contains a sizable amount of unfermented sugar. The following spring the new wine is transported from *quintas,* or vineyard estates, along the Douro, to warehouses (called lodges) in Vila Nova de Gaia, where it is aged in wood for several years. Young Port is very agreeable—sweet with a pronounced grapey taste—but it has not yet developed much breed or character.

A Ruby Port is characterized by a rich color and a fruity and distinctive taste. A Tawny Port has a somewhat lighter color, its taste is somewhat drier, and it has a more refined and delicate character. A Tawny is not necessarily much older than a Ruby, because its paler color and lighter body can be arranged by blending in some white Port. These wood-aged Ports account for almost all of the Ports shipped to this country, but every so often, perhaps three times in a decade, the Port shippers "declare a vintage," that is, they judge the year's crop good enough to remain unblended with wines of other years. The result is Vintage Port, which is handled differently, and which some experts consider to be the finest wine produced anywhere. A Vintage Port is aged in wood for less than three years, then bottled. The bottling usually takes place in England, because that is where the wine will be consumed. Because aging in glass is slower than in wood, Vintage Ports usually need fifteen or twenty years before they can be drunk with pleasure, and forty or fifty years is not too old for this wine. The sediment that would normally develop in wood now develops in the bottle, and well-aged Vintage Ports are characterized by a "crust" that makes careful decanting a necessity. A Vintage Port properly served is a wine of tremendous style, but it is not often seen here. A bottle labeled "Port of the Vintage . . ." with a year, refers only to an unblended Tawny Port, that is, a wood-aged Port of that particular year.

White Port is about as sweet as a red Port, and is becoming popular as an aperitif, chilled or on ice.

Among the brands found in this country whose names testify to the influence of the English on the Port trade, are Cockburns, Croft, Dow, Harveys, Hooper's, Osborne, Robertson, Sandeman and Taylor's.

California Ports are widely available and vary widely in quality. The best of them are full, fruity, mellow wines that nevertheless lack the subtlety and complexity of the wines from the Douro. Port made in New York State tends to retain more of the native *labrusca* flavor than does Sherry.

MADEIRA AND MARSALA

Madeira is a small Portuguese island off the coast of North Africa whose distinctive fortified wines range from fairly dry to very sweet. In Colonial times, Madeira was probably the most popular wine in America, and was specially imported by the best families of Boston, New York, and Charleston, but only a small quantity is imported today. The vineyards of Madeira were devastated by two plagues in the second half of the nineteenth century, first the fungus oïdium, then phylloxera, and its production has never regained its former size.

When Madeira is vinified, the point at which fermentation is stopped depends upon how sweet or dry the finished wine is meant to be, so that more or less unfermented sugar is retained. As is the case with Port, the fermentation of sweet Madeira is halted in mid-course by the addition of brandy, but dry Madeiras are completely fermented, just like Sherry. The fortified wines are then put in rooms called *estufas,* or ovens, and the wines are slowly baked for several months. This concentrated aging process is meant to approximate the beneficial effects of a long sea voyage, as it was discovered in the eighteenth century that the long voyages to which all cargo was subjected seemed to improve the wines of Madeira.

Madeira has a special pungent taste that comes from the volcanic soil in which the vines are planted, as well as an agreeable cooked or burned taste that it acquires in the *estufas.* Sercial is the driest of all Madeiras, Malmsey the sweetest, with Verdelho and Bual, or Boal, bridging the gap. Rainwater Madeira, typically pale in color, is now used as a generic name, and may be more or less sweet according to the dictates of each shipper. Madeira is among the longest-lived of all wines, and it is still possible to find some fifty- or one-hundred-year-old Madeiras in some shops in major cities: good examples of these wines are by no means faded, and offer a remarkable tasting experience.

Marsala is a fortified wine made in Sicily. As is the case with Sherry, the wine is completely fermented until it is dry, then later fortified and sweetened. (Even dry Marsala is not very dry.) Most firms market not only a sweet Marsala, but specially flavored Marsalas as well, using egg yolks, almonds, and so forth.

Málaga, not often encountered here, is a sweet, brown fortified wine from the city of that name in southern Spain.

VERMOUTH AND APERITIFS

Vermouth, both sweet and dry, is most often used in mixed drinks, but it is also popular as an aperitif, and is usually served with ice and a twist of lemon peel. Vermouth has a wine base, and is fortified, sweetened, and flavored with various herbs and spices according to each firm's secret recipe. Traditionally, Italian Vermouth is red and sweet, while French Vermouth is pale and dry, but both types are made in both countries, and about half of the Vermouth sold here is made in this country. The French town of Chambéry, near the Swiss-Italian border, has given its name to a distinctive pale and dry Vermouth.

Anything that is drunk before a meal—Sherry, Vermouth, white wine, Champagne, or even a cocktail—could properly be described as an aperitif, but the term aperitif wine usually refers to certain proprietary names, such as Dubonnet, St. Raphaël, Byrrh, and Lillet. They are mostly red and are made more or less like sweet Vermouth, although their flavor is more pronounced and distinctive, because they are meant to be drunk by themselves, with ice and perhaps a splash of soda water. Quinine is often one of the ingredients, and it contributes a slightly bitter aftertaste that tempers the sweetness of the aperitif.

Cognac and
Other Brandies

ALTHOUGH this book is primarily concerned with wine, a meal at which good wines are served often ends with a glass of brandy, which is simply distilled wine. The word is derived from *brandewijn,* a Dutch word for burned (distilled) wine. Wherever grapes are grown and made into wine, brandy of some kind is also made. The most famous and most highly regarded of all brandies is Cognac, which is distilled from wine produced in a specifically delimited area in southwest France, about seventy miles north of Bordeaux. All Cognac is brandy, but there is only one brandy that can be called Cognac.

It was in the early seventeenth century that the white wines produced in the valley of the Charente River were first distilled to make a *vin brûlé,* presumably to provide an alcoholic beverage that would be less bulky to ship than wine. The city of Cognac, which lies on the bank of the Charente, gave its name to this brandy in the eighteenth century, and only as recently as a hundred years ago did the various Cognac producers first begin to bottle and label their brandy in their own cellars, thus establishing the brand names by which almost all Cognac is recognized today.

We have seen how important soil is to the quality and characteristics of various wines, and this is equally true for Cognac, which has been poetically described as "the soul of wine." There are seven sharply defined districts whose wines are permitted to be distilled into Cognac. The two most important inner districts are called Grande Champagne and Petite Champagne, but these names bear no relation to the sparkling wines of Champagne. Champagne in French means open fields, a distinction made even clearer by considering the names of the five other districts, four of which refer to woodlands: Borderies, Fins Bois, Bons Bois, Bois Ordinaires, and Bois Communs. These legally delimited areas were established when it was discovered that the wines from each district, when distilled, produced Cognacs with marked differences in quality: the very best Cognacs come from Grande Champagne and Petite Champagne.

There are three grape varieties used to make Charente wines, but it is the Saint-Emilion (also known as the Ugni Blanc, and unrelated to the Bordeaux wine district) that has gradually replaced the Folle Blanche and the Colombard. The white wine of the Charente is thin and sour, usually under 10 percent in alcohol, and unattractive to drink. Oddly enough, the wine produced in Grande Champagne from its predominantly chalky soil tastes even worse than the rest, and yet it produces the finest Cognac. There are no quantity limits per acre to the wines produced in the Charente, but the growers vinify their wines carefully, because any off-taste or defect in the wine will show up even more strongly in the distilled brandy. Much of the annual wine crop is sold directly to big distilling houses that are owned or under contract to the biggest Cognac shippers, but many thousands of small growers also distill their own Cognac, to be sold later to the shippers.

Once the wine has been made, distillation takes place in old-fashioned pot stills, which resemble giant copper kettles, and proceeds for several months on a twenty-four-hour schedule. The small grower-distillers move their beds near their pot stills and maintain a steady vigil over the distillation process. Cognac is unusual in that it is doubly distilled. The first distillation produces a liquid of about 60° proof (or 30 percent alcohol), called *brouillis*. This is redistilled to make the raw Cognac, known as the *bonne chauffe*, which comes out of the still at 140° proof. It takes about ten barrels of wine to make a barrel of Cognac. Distillation is deliberately slow, so that the characteristics of the wine are imparted to the brandy. These congeners, or impurities, give a brandy its particular character, and a fast, high-proof distillation would result in a relatively flavorless alcohol.

The raw Cognac, which is colorless, is then aged in oak

barrels made from Limousin oak. It is the interaction between oak and brandy, as well as the continual oxidation
that takes place through the porous wood, that gives Cognac its superb and distinctive flavor. The basic elements
are present in embryonic form in the raw Cognac, but it
is barrel-aging (during which the brandy picks up color and
tannin from the oak) that refines a harsh distillate into an
inimitable beverage.

Aging is expensive, however, not only because the millions of gallons of Cognac lying in the warehouses of the
big shippers and in small cellars throughout the country-
side represent an enormous capital outlay, but also because
Cognac evaporates as it ages. It is claimed that as much
Cognac evaporates into the atmosphere every day as is
consumed in France, and this "angel's drink" adds to the
final cost of an old Cognac. The finest Cognacs will continue to improve in barrel for about forty years, after
which there is a danger that they will dry out and take on
a woody, or stalky flavor. Very old Cognacs are therefore
stored in glass demijohns, because brandy does not change
once it is put into glass. Cognacs from lesser districts, on the
other hand, will mature and mellow for only a few years,
at which time they are already quite pleasant. They can
naturally be improved by being combined with older Cognacs from other districts, and it is at this point that the
blender's skill comes into play. Apart from Cognacs that
may have been distilled especially for them, all the Cognac
houses constantly buy young Cognacs from the thousands
of grower-distillers in the region. Tremendous stocks of
different Cognacs of different ages must be maintained by
the shippers in order to make up their respective house
styles on a continuous basis. For example, a Cognac from
Grande Champagne will eventually have a tremendous
bouquet and outstanding breed and finesse, but it will take
many years in wood before it can be used alone. Combined
with other Cognacs that are perhaps less fine in themselves
but have certain balancing attributes, a blend that needs
less age can be made and can be sold for considerably less
than an unblended Grande Champagne.

As Cognac ages, its alcoholic content diminishes slowly,
but it is obviously not possible to age every Cognac until
it arrives at a marketable strength—usually around 80°

proof—and the shippers must therefore add distilled water to their final blends to achieve the desired proof.

Although Cognac takes on color from the oak as it matures, its pale brown color will vary according to age and the kind of barrel used and is invariably augmented with harmless caramel coloring before being bottled, so that every bottle will look the same.

There are a number of markings that traditionally appear on Cognac labels, and some of these are more meaningful than others. A Grande Champagne Cognac or Grande Fine Champagne Cognac has been made entirely from wines whose grapes were grown in the Grande Champagne district, and this is the highest appellation possible. More familiar is Fine Champagne Cognac, which indicates that the brandy comes from both Grande and Petite Champagne, with at least 50 percent from Grande Champagne.

The stars and letters on labels have less specific meanings. Most Cognac shippers market three grades—a 5-Star (or 3-Star), a VSOP (Very Superior Old Pale), and in limited quantities, something a bit special that may be called Extra, Triomphe, Cordon Bleu, XO, or the like. These are all relative terms referring to age and have no legal correlation to the amount of years spent in barrel. Each individual house will naturally make its Extra older than its VSOP, which is in turn older than its 5-Star. But there is nothing to prevent a shipper from making his VSOP only four years old (the French legal minimum) and to put his fanciest label on, say, a six-year-old brandy. It is for this reason that the name of the shipper is especially important when buying Cognac.

Other letters seen on Cognac labels include VO (Very Old), VVSOP, (Very Very Superior Old Pale), VSEP, (Very Superior Extra/Especially Pale). That these initials refer to English words indicates the great importance that the English market has always had for the Cognac trade. As the worldwide demand for Cognac has increased, and as the amount of wine produced in Charente remains more or less fixed, the step in production that has had to give is the amount of aging in wood, in order to provide more bottles for existing markets. As a result, the guidelines usually given to equate stars and initials to age are, I believe, no longer valid. Cognac tastings are too expensive to contemplate, but if you enjoy a good Cognac, why not compare two or three brands next time you dine out with friends in a good restaurant? Remember also that unless you drink brandy and soda (a most enjoyable highball, by the way), you will do better to spend an extra dollar or two to buy a firm's VSOP. The taxes are so high even on a 5-Star Cognac that the incremental cost for better quality is minimal compared to the increase in enjoyment.

It is rare to see the age of a Cognac in this country, as the French government will not guarantee age on its export certificates beyond five years. Furthermore, even vintage Cognacs have been evaporating in barrel over the years and have probably been refreshed with younger Cognacs. Finally, a word about Napoleon Cognacs that supposedly date from his day. If you came across a bottle dated, say, 1812, you would have no way of knowing how long the brandy had spent in wood. If the Cognac had been bottled in 1813, it would simply be a one-year-old Cognac, for once in bottle brandies no longer improve.

Cognac is most often served in special brandy glasses, which are available in a variety of sizes. It is traditional to cup the bowl with your palm, so that the applied warmth releases the brandy's bouquet. For this reason very small and very big glasses are less comfortable than those with a bowl whose size is somewhere between that of a tangerine and an apple. Good Cognac is noted for its complex and refined bouquet, and in fact brandy glasses are also known as snifters. A professional Cognac taster actually relies more on his nose than on his palate when buying young Cognacs or making a final blend, and if you pause a moment to inhale Cognac before tasting it, you'll be surprised at how much this will tell you about its style and quality.

Among the leading Cognac firms, listed alphabetically, are

Bisquit	Martell
Courvoisier	Monnet
Delamain	Otard
Denis-Mounie	Polignac
Gaston de Lagrange	Remy Martin
Hennessy	Salignac
Hine	

Cognac may be the most famous of all brandies, but there are quite a few others that serve admirably to round out a meal. After Cognac, the best known of all French brandies is Armagnac, which is somewhat richer and fuller in taste than Cognac. If it lacks the finesse and distinction of Cognac at its very best, Armagnac nevertheless offers excellent value: it ages more quickly than Cognac, and comparatively priced examples may therefore be softer and mellower.

Armagnac comes from southwest France, from a region near the Pyrenees that used to be called Gascony. The region is not widely traveled, and the inhabitants are determined individualists, with long memories for local history. When they speak of "the occupation" they usually mean the occupation of Gascony by the English in the fifteenth century. And how many people would display, as a proud exhibit in their local museum, a *bidon de fraudeur,* a flat metal container shaped to fit against a man's stomach, and used for smuggling Armagnac under one's clothes. Because Armagnac has never achieved the popularity of Cognac, production is not dominated by a few important shipping houses as it is in Cognac, and a great many small farmers have barrels of Armagnac aging in their cellars or behind the barn. These farmers can produce brandy, despite their limited facilities, because of a most unusual feature of the distillation process. The stills are not individually owned by the producers, as in Cognac, but are mounted on wheels, and travel throughout the region transforming wine into Armagnac from November through the following April. These portable stills, which resemble small locomotives, enable anyone who makes wine to make Armagnac as well. As in Cognac, the white wine from the Armagnac region is thin and meager. It is also characterized by a special earthy taste, which finds its way into the brandy in a subdued form, and this is a basic characteristic of the taste of Armagnac. Distillation of Armagnac is one continual process (Cognac is twice-distilled) and the brandy trickles from the still at an average of 104° proof (whereas Cognac is distilled at 140° proof). This means that more of the original taste of the wine "comes over" during distillation, giving the brandy a more pronounced character. Armagnac is then aged in black Gascon oak from the local forests. This oak imparts more flavor to the brandy than does, for example, the Limousin oak used to mature Cognac, and the brandy matures more quickly.

Armagnac is usually bottled in the *basquaise* bottle, a round, flat bottle similar to that used for Chilean wines. No brands dominate the market, but conversely, some of the finest Armagnacs from smaller *domaines* are available in this country.

A brandy that provokes strong feelings pro and con is marc (pronounced *mar*), which is also produced in Italy as grappa. Marc is the residue of skins, pits, and stalks from which wine has been pressed out. Water is added to the marc, left to referment, and this mixture is then distilled to produce a very pungent and distinctive brandy. The best known marc is Marc de Bourgogne, although the brandy is also produced in Champagne and in the Rhone Valley. Although it seems logical that this brandy could be made successfully from any leftover pressed grapes, experiment indicates otherwise. Marc is not distilled in Bordeaux, for example. The director of one world-famous vineyard has tried to produce a marc for years, knowing sales would be immediate, but he admits that the resulting brandy is "too horrible to bottle," and sells it off as industrial alcohol.

Marc, which has a strawlike bouquet and somewhat leathery taste, is occasionally made from pressings of a particular vineyard and so labeled, such as Marc de Chambertin or Marc de la Romanée-Conti.

The grappa of Italy is colorless, and seems to lack the mellowness of the best French marc.

Spanish brandy is popular here, notably the Fundador of Pedro Domecq. The brandy is distilled from various wines and blended in Jerez, which is most famous, of course, for its Sherry. Spanish brandies seem sweeter and richer in taste than those from France, and are quite mellow to the palate. Greek brandies are imported in small quantities. The best known of them has a sweet, rich, almost honeyed flavor that is quite special. Asbach Uralt is the biggest seller here among German imports; it is a delicate and attractive brandy in the French style.

The United States produces three-quarters of all the brandy consumed in this country, and almost all of this comes from California. California brandy is usually a bit sweeter in taste and less complex in flavor than the better imports, but it is also less expensive.

Among the nongrape brandies, the most unusual, often the most expensive, and to some palates the finest of all brandies, are those distilled from wild fruits in the mountains of Alsace and Switzerland and in the Black Forest of Germany. They are produced in very small quantities, and restaurateurs in France and Germany compete with a few importers for the finest examples. *Kirsch* (wild cherry), *framboise* (wild raspberry), *mirabelle* (yellow plum), *quetsch* (purple plum), and *poire* (pear) are the best known, and because they are colorless, they are known generically as *alcools blancs,* or white alcohols. Actually, all distillates are colorless when they come from the still, but we seem to be more comfortable if whiskies, rum, and most brandies are pale brown, although we accept gin and vodka in their natural state.

The *alcools blancs* are made in a special way. The wild fruit is macerated in wooden tubs and left to ferment, i.e. the sugar is transformed into alcohol, without which there would be nothing to distill. In the case of pit fruits, some of the pits are also crushed, releasing an oil that gives a characteristic undertaste to the brandy. A great deal of fruit is needed to produce a bottle of brandy—between fifteen and thirty pounds of raspberries are needed to make a bottle of *framboise*—which is why these brandies are so expensive. Once fermented, the mash is distilled and the brandy is left for a few months or a couple of years (every producer has his own preferences) in white wood, which does not impart any color to the distillate. The brandy is later transferred to porcelain jars until ready for bottling. Although most brandy undergoes absolutely no change once it has been transferred from wood to glass, it is believed that white alcohols do mellow in porcelain and that their bouquets continue to develop. Some producers of these fruit brandies claim that they should be served chilled: their extraordinary bouquet does not seem to suffer and they are smoother if swallowed cold. In any event, it is the delicate and fragrant bouquet of these white alcohols, each reminiscent of the original fruit in its ripe and undistilled state, that makes these brandies so remarkable and so different from grape brandies.

Fruit brandies are distilled at 100° proof and sold at around 90° proof: for all their haunting bouquet they are by no means bland. These *alcools blancs* bear no relation to various fruit-flavored brandies, such as blackberry brandy or apricot brandy, which are made in an entirely different way and especially sweetened.

Another famous fruit brandy is Calvados, made from apple cider in the French *départment* of Calvados, in Normandy. The best Calvados comes from the Pays d'Auge, which produces the best cider. When properly aged, Calvados is a delicious brandy, with a distinctive applelike tang. A local custom is the *trou Normand*—a pause in the middle of a long dinner to swallow a shot of Calvados, which supposedly aids the digestion and makes room for the rich courses to follow. Applejack is the American equivalent of Calvados: the main difference seems to be that it's not aged as long and has less of an apple taste to it.

When the moment is at hand for an after-dinner brandy, there is certainly no lack of choice. If you hesitate to buy a full bottle of an unfamiliar brandy, the best way to experiment is to try different brandies in restaurants. Those restaurants that feature other than American cuisine usually have one or two of the less familiar imported brandies to match. You're bound to discover something new that is very much to your taste.

The Enjoyment of Wine

BUYING AND STORING WINES

ALTHOUGH every liquor store or wine outlet carries at least a limited selection of wines from several countries, there is such a great variety of wines available and at so many different prices that it's well worth your while to shop around. There are in almost every city several stores whose proprietor is fully aware of the growing consumer interest in wines, and who makes an effort to have a large selection of well-chosen wines from a variety of sources. There you will find wines from many countries at different prices, including those of the most famous vineyards in good vintages. Another advantage of seeking out a wine-conscious retailer is that he may periodically issue a catalog listing his wines, which you can study at your leisure. If there is any homework that a wine enthusiast can assign himself, apart from drinking wine regularly, it is to spend some free moments looking through wine catalogs. This will enlarge your awareness of what is actually available to drink and at what prices, and it also permits you to look up any unfamiliar wine names, which you can not do when you're standing in front of a bottle on a shelf. If you live in a big city with several good wine stores, get on their mailing lists. If the choice is limited in your own town, at least remember to pick up a catalog or two when you travel, for reference purposes.

Once you've found a good wine source or two, try to find a corner in your home that you can use as a wine cellar. This needn't be elaborate, and you might start with only half-a-dozen bottles, but there are several reasons why it pays to buy wines ahead of time. For one thing, you don't have to run out at the last minute if guests are expected, nor will you find yourself with no wine left halfway through dinner. For another, you don't have to rely on the corner liquor store, which can be especially annoying if you've already discovered that the selection is limited and the prices high. Also, good red wines need at least a few days' rest to taste their best once they've been shaken up. If you have a few such wines on hand, you'll be sure of getting the most they have to offer. Finally, don't underestimate the real pleasure of being able to choose a wine from your own cellar—red, white, or rosé—that suits your dinner and your mood.

The cellar itself can be as simple as a whiskey carton turned on its side, and the guides to maintaining a store of wines are simple and logical. The first rule, of course, is to lay a wine bottle on its side, so that the cork is kept moist and expanded, preventing air from entering the bottle. Ideally, wines should be kept at a constant 55° to 60°, away from daylight and vibrations. These conditions can obviously be met only by those who have access to a real cellar, which most of us do not. To keep wines in a home or apartment, you should remember that evenness of temperature is at least as important as the temperature itself, within limitations, because constant fluctuations of heat and cold will hasten a wine's maturation and eventual decline. Therefore, keep wines away from boiler rooms, steam pipes, or kitchen ovens. Don't store wines in a place where they will be subject to a lot of knocking about, such as the closet where the brooms and vacuum cleaner are kept. And keep wines away from direct exposure to daylight, which seems to decompose them in a short time (whether in your house or in a retailer's window). If the temperature of your cellar stays much above 70°, you should limit yourself to no more than a six months' supply of wines. With these general rules in mind, you should be able to figure out a good place to store a few bottles.

Wine racks are available from most department stores and, in many states, from liquor stores. Many of these racks are designed to be stacked, and you should look for these, so that you can expand the capacity of your cellar.

Never buy racks in which the bottles lie at a downward angle, neck lowest. The cork will be kept moistened, but any sediment in fine red wines will slide toward the cork and may adhere to it. You will thus drink cloudy wine from your first glass.

As you determine the wines you enjoy the most, you will want to increase your cellar. For one thing, buying wines by the case of twelve bottles will usually save you 10 percent. For another, the better wines of Bordeaux and Burgundy are cheapest in each vintage when they first appear on the market, and then gradually increase in price: sometimes not so gradually, if the vintage is highly publicized or in short supply.

A lot has been written recently about wine as an investment. The first thing to understand is that if you buy good wines of a good vintage when they are first offered, you will almost certainly save money as their retail cost increases over the years. But you will not make money because it is illegal for a consumer, without the necessary licenses, to resell wine. In any case, the only wines whose value consistently increases are classified red Bordeaux, and especially the first growths, which are expensive to begin with. Red Burgundies do not increase in value as rapidly, but it is nevertheless wise to buy them because, being scarce, wines from the best vineyards often disappear within a couple of years. This is also true of Cabernet Sauvignon from the best California wineries. Needless to say, imported wines of poor vintages are not to be bought carelessly, much less stored away. A number of larger liquor stores will store cases of wine for their customers for a nominal fee.

A Beginning Wine Cellar

The following list of wines has been divided into a dozen or so categories, according to place of origin and price. This selection can be used simply as a quick checklist when you buy a few bottles, or you can choose two wines from each category, which will give you a beginning wine cellar of about thirty different wines at a cost of one hundred dollars or so.

To expand your cellar and your taste, you might at first choose more wines from each category—there is variety enough among districts and vineyards and among brands and shippers. In time, as you determine which wines you find most enjoyable, you can concentrate on fewer categories and build up a collection that more closely corresponds to your own preferences.

If you want to add some of the most famous wines to your cellar, look for good vintages of the first growths of Bordeaux (priced at ten to twenty dollars), the *grand crû* vineyards of Burgundy (eight to fifteen dollars), and the finest Spätlese and Auslese wines of the Rhine and Moselle (five to ten dollars). These wines, as well as all of the wines listed below, are described in the text and can be found in the index.

FRANCE

Red Bordeaux: Regional wines from the Médoc, Saint-Emilion, Saint-Julien, Margaux, or Saint-Estèphe; or *petits châteaux* from these regions, or from Fronsac, Bourg, or Blaye. $2.–3.50

Red Bordeaux: Individual vineyard wines from such classified *châteaux* as: $4.–7.

Léoville-Las-Cases	Trotanoy
Lascombes	Beychevelle
Montrose	Prieuré-Lichine
Palmer	Troplong-Mondot
Calon-Ségur	Figeac
Talbot	Pape-Clément
l'Evangile	Nénin
Grand-Puy-Lacoste	Pichon-Lalande

Beaujolais: Beaujolais, Beaujolais-Villages, or better yet, some of the Beaujolais *crûs* such as Brouilly, Fleurie, Juliénas, or Moulin-à-Vent. $2.50–3.50

Red Burgundy: Village wines from the Côte de Nuits or the Côte de Beaune such as Gevrey-Chambertin, Vosne-Romanée, Nuits-Saint-Georges, Aloxe-Corton, Beaune, Pommard, Volnay. $4.–7.

White Burgundy: Chablis or Pouilly-Fuissé or village wines from the Côte de Beaune such as Chassagne-Montrachet, Puligny-Montrachet, Meursault. $3.–5.

Other White Wines: $2.–3.50
Burgundy: Pinot Chardonnay or Mâcon Blanc.
Bordeaux: Graves (dry) or Sauternes/Barsac (sweet).
Loire: Muscadet, Sancerre, Pouilly-Fumé, Vouvray.
Alsace: Riesling, Gewürztraminer.

ITALY

Red Wines: Chianti Classico, Bardolino, Valpolicella, Barolo. $2.50–3.50

White Wines: Soave, Verdicchio, Lacrima Christi,
Orvieto, Frascati. $2.–3.

GERMANY

Regional wines such as Liebfraumilch, Bernkasteler, Piesporter, Niersteiner Domtal, and Johannisberger Riesling are available at all prices. The
best-known brands cost $2.50–3.50

The best German wines come from individual
vineyards and are estate-bottled. Here are some of
the better village names, to which an individual
vineyard name should be appended, i.e., Rauen-
thaler Baiken, Bernkasteler Badstube, Piesporter
Goldtröpfchen. $3.–4.50

Rhine: Forst, Oppenheim, Eltville, Rauenthal,
Johannisberg, Hattenheim.

Moselle-Saar-Ruwer: Wehlen, Zeltingen, Bernkastel, Piesport, Brauneberg, Ockfen, Kasel.

OTHER COUNTRIES

Red Wines $2.–3.
Spain: Rioja, Valdepeñas.
Portugal: Dão.
Hungary: Egri Bikavér.
Yugoslavia: Cabernet, Pinot Noir.
Chile: Pinot.
United States (*California*): Cabernet Sauvignon,
Pinot Noir, Gamay, Zinfandel. $2.–3.50
White Wines $2.–3.
Portugal: Vinho Verde.
Switzerland: Neuchâtel, Fendant du Valais.
Austria: Gumpoldskirchner, Grinzinger.
Yugoslavia: Riesling, Traminer.

Chile: Riesling.
United States (*California*): Chardonnay, Johannis-
    berg Riesling, Chenin Blanc, Sauvignon Blanc,
    Sémillon. $2.–3.50

Rosés—readily available from many countries—include Rosé
d'Anjou, Tavel and Provence rosés from France; the Lake
Garda rosés from Italy; a number of brands in distinctive bottles from Portugal; and Grenache Rosé and Gamay Rosé from
California.

To complete a small cellar you might want to add one or two
bottles of Champagne or sparkling wine; a bottle of dry or
sweet Sherry; perhaps a Tawny or Ruby Port; and a bottle
of Cognac or other brandy.

SERVING WINES

Serving wine—or more specifically, drinking wine—is certainly not very complicated and can be briefly summarized:
chill white wines and rosés; open red wines half an hour
before pouring them, and serve them at room temperature;
use large, stemmed glasses that are slightly tapered, and
fill them only halfway. This covers the subject in a general
way and gets you started as a wine drinker. There is so
much conversation and snobbism about the proper way to
drink wines, however, that it might be useful to describe
the various steps in serving a wine. What follows is not
meant to discourage anyone by its attention to detail, but
rather to indicate, for reference, the most logical way to
approach every aspect of getting a wine from the cellar
into your glass. The degree of special effort to be made will
depend on the wine and the occasion: a sandwich doesn't
need a special presentation, nor is an elaborately prepared
dish best served on paper plates.
    Older red wines, which may throw a slight and harmless
deposit, should be stood upright on the dining table or side-
board an hour or two before the meal to permit any sediment to slide to the bottom. Red wines are supposed to be
served at room temperature, which is to say, not at the
cooler temperature of the ideal cellar. Because few of us

have cellars, the bottle has presumably been lying in a closet or in a rack along the wall, so the wine is already at room temperature. Historically, room temperature referred to dining rooms without central heating, and actually red wines don't taste their best if served too warm, much above 70°, say, no matter what the temperature of the room is. In the summer it's advisable to cool down a light red wine (Beaujolais, California Burgundy, Bardolino) by putting it in the refrigerator for twenty minutes or so. This will give the wine an agreeable freshness and actually seems to improve its flavor. A complex red wine, however, should never be chilled, nor should any red wine be warmed near a fire or oven: the wine will be numbed, and it will have neither bouquet nor flavor.

White wines and rosés are served chilled, because it is their refreshing quality that is their greatest virtue. Two hours in the refrigerator will do the job. If you need a chilled bottle of white wine at the last minute or a second bottle to serve with a dinner in progress, empty one or two ice trays into your biggest cooking pot, fill it with water, and put in the bottle. It should be cool in fifteen or twenty minutes. The trouble with most wine coolers or ice buckets is that they are too shallow and chill only half the bottle. Chilling a wine in ice water is both quicker and safer than putting the bottle in the freezer. The colder a wine is, the harder it is to taste, and some people use the trick of overchilling a poor bottle of white wine to mask its defects. For the same reason, a fine bottle of Sauternes or a rich German wine should not be chilled too much, or you will deaden the qualities for which you have paid.

A corkscrew is really the only piece of equipment that a wine drinker needs, and as it will last for years, it pays to look for a good one. In the first place, the screw part, called the bore, should be at least two inches long. Because good wines are long-lived, they are bottled with long, strong corks, and a poor corkscrew will invariably break the cork of every expensive bottle of wine that you buy. Secondly, the bore should be in the form of a true coil, not a wiggly line. A coil will get a real grip even on an old cork, whereas a wiggly line will just bore a hole in it. Finally, get a corkscrew that gives you leverage. A simple T-shaped corkscrew, even with an excellent bore, requires

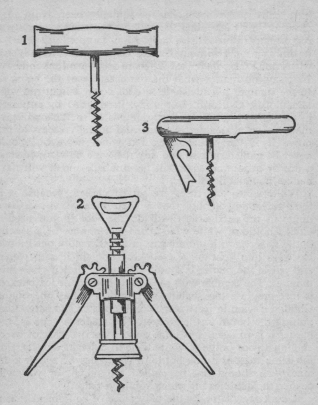

CORKSCREWS

A good corkscrew should have a "worm" at least two inches long with smooth edges, so that it can completely penetrate a long cork without crumbling it. The worm should also be in the form of a real coil, rather than having an awllike solid core: a corkscrew must be able to grip an old cork, not drill a hole in it. The simplest corkscrew (1) may require some awkward tugging; a corkscrew with some kind of leverage action (such as 2) is usually more convenient. The folding corkscrew (3) is favored by waiters because it can be carried in a pocket and its leverage action enables it to be used on a bottle lying on its side in a wine basket.

too much tugging, and you will find yourself gripping the bottle between your feet or your knees, which can lead to messy accidents.

To open a bottle of wine, first remove the lead foil that covers the cork and part of the neck. Because lead foil may have an unpleasant taste, cut it off well below the lip of the bottle, so that the wine will not be in contact with the foil as it's poured. Wipe off the top of the cork and insert the corkscrew into the center of the cork. Remember to pull the cork gently, because if you give it a sharp tug, the vacuum that is momentarily created between the wine and the rising cork may cause some wine to splash out of the bottle.

If you break the cork, and this occasionally happens even with a bottle of sound wine, reinsert the corkscrew at an angle to get a grip on the remaining piece. If the cork crumbles, you can simply strain the wine into another container through clear cheesecloth or a tea strainer.

Incidentally, you should never wrap a wine bottle in a napkin: it's considered bad manners not to let your guests see what is being poured into their glasses. If you're worried that a few drops of wine may spill onto the tablecloth, you can tie a small napkin around the neck of the bottle.

A red wine should be opened about half an hour before you plan to pour it. This additional exposure to air, called breathing, will develop its bouquet and soften the character of a young, firm wine. This is particularly useful for a fine wine that you suspect is not yet fully mature: a little breathing will deepen its flavor and make it less harsh to the palate. You will often discover in a restaurant that the second glass of a good red wine tastes better than the first, and that is precisely because the extra exposure to air has hastened its development. Certain wines, especially older Burgundies, take on a slight off-odor when they are first opened, perhaps the result of their long imprisonment in the bottle. A little breathing will dissipate this unwiny bouquet.

It's customary in a restaurant for the host to taste the first glass of wine in case a bad bottle has been served or to prevent any bits of cork from reaching the glasses of his guests. This seems to me unnecessary in one's home, because you should taste the wine when you open it. There's no more logic to first tasting a wine when everyone is seated than for a cook to first taste a sauce after it's been served to her guests. (Imagine the awkward scramble if the bottle is defective.) What's more, if you taste a red wine when you uncork it, you lower the level of the wine below the neck, exposing a greater surface of wine to air, and thus hastening the effects of breathing.

Decanting red wines may seem complicated or affected or both, but it's very simple and very useful. The sediment that older red wines develop after ten years or so, although harmless, is also distracting when it appears in the last two or three glasses that are poured. Decanting a wine, which simply involves transferring it from its original bottle to another container, permits you to serve a wine that is completely brilliant and unclouded to the very end, and at the sacrifice of only an ounce or two of wine. First, you must stand the bottle up for at least two hours to allow all the sediment to fall to the bottom. When you open the bottle, remove all of the foil, so that you get an unobstructed view of the wine as it pours out through the neck of the bottle. Your decanter can be any clean container, whether it's a crystal wine decanter, an empty bottle, or a glass pitcher. Hold the decanter firmly (remember, it will soon contain a full bottle of wine) and transfer the wine slowly in one motion—otherwise the sediment will wash back and forth. Traditionally, the neck of the wine bottle is held over a candle, so that you can see when sediment begins to come over into the decanter and can stop pouring at that moment. Because we now have electricity and because the heat of a candle is not going to do an old wine any good, you can just as easily pour against a bright light or bare bulb.

If you are worried about decanting a ten-dollar bottle of wine, decant the next wine you drink, whatever it is, just to get the hang of it. Decanting is not only the best way to get your money's worth out of older wines, when you can afford them, but it also seems to be a much simpler way of letting young wines breathe, as decanting exposes a wine to more air more quickly than simply pulling its cork. A decanter of wine on a dining table is also a most attractive and appropriate decoration and enhances the enjoyment of wine. If you're concerned that a good wine will go unnoticed because it's unlabeled, you should know that it's customary to put the empty bottle alongside the decanter, so that your guests will know what they're drinking.

Decanting wine is also useful if you're bringing wine to a restaurant that permits this or to a friend's house. Of course you can buy a bottle on the way over, but occasionally you may want to bring over a good bottle from your own cellar. A useful trick is to decant the wine into any container, rinse out the bottle, and then pour the wine back in and cork it up. This gives you wine without sediment, allows the wine to breathe, and saves you the bother of trying to transport the wine gently, without shaking up any sediment.

There is one other point about decanting, which may seem finicky, but remember, you've got an old bottle that cost you several dollars, and you want to get the most out of it. Because these bottles don't come our way very often, your decanter may be musty or have an off-odor from whatever was in it last. Therefore, you might first pour a few drops of wine into the decanter, rinse, and pour it out. This will not only remove any odor that may be in the decanter, but will give the decanter the bouquet of the wine that's about to go into it.

Wine glasses have been discussed earlier, in the chapter on tasting, but to summarize: use a stemmed, clear glass with a bowl the shape of an elongated U, slightly tapered at the top to retain the wine's bouquet, and with a capacity of at least eight ounces. Small glasses seem stingy, and don't permit a wine to be swirled to release its bouquet. Glasses with tall stems and colored bowls are sometimes recommended for German wines, but they only hide the delicate golden colors of a fine Moselle or Rhine wine. These glasses originated when wine-making techniques had not been perfected, and a finished wine was apt to turn cloudy. Colored bowls hid this defect.

Almost every major wine region has its traditional glass, just as it has its traditional bottle, but it is completely unnecessary to have different glasses to properly serve and enjoy wine. When two or more wines are served at a meal, it does dress up the table to use differently shaped glasses, but even here an all-purpose wine glass is perfectly acceptable. If you do use glasses of two different sizes, the smaller one is used for white wines, the larger for reds. If you serve

WINE GLASSES

The ten-ounce all-purpose wine glass (1) can be used for all
table wines, as well as for Sherry, Port, or Champagne, if need
be. It should never be filled more than halfway, so that the
wine can be swirled to release its bouquet. The first glass is in
the traditional Bordeaux shape; the second all-purpose glass (2)
is in the traditional Burgundy shape and would preferably be
used only for table wines. The classic Champagne glass (3)
displays bubbles more attractively and releases them more slowly
than does the familiar saucer glass. The traditional brandy glass
(4) may vary in capacity from about six to twelve ounces:
a much smaller or much bigger glass will be difficult to cup in
one's hand, as is done to release the brandy's bouquet.

two reds, the better wine should be poured into the bigger glass.

As a general rule, expensive red wines will not keep a second day, and you had better plan to drink them when opened. Their flavor tends to become somewhat muddy and dulled, at best, and may taste rather sharp and vinegary at worst. Almost all white wines can usually be kept in the refrigerator for several days and are only slightly the worse for wear. Inexpensive red and white wines, especially those from California, will keep much better, because they have been treated to remain more stable once they're exposed to air. It doesn't hurt to keep even the red wines in the refrigerator, or at least in a cool place, just as you would with milk or any other perishable product.

The most helpful point to remember about leftover wine is to cork it up immediately after dinner—it doesn't help a half-empty bottle of wine to be left open an extra hour or two.

When you put the cork back into a bottle for any reason, remember not to put the top, which is usually dirty, in contact with the wine. If the bottom of the cork has expanded, once pulled, and can not easily be replaced, the simplest solution is to slice one-fourth inch off the top and then reverse it.

If you do find yourself with leftover wine that is still drinkable but which may have lost some of its flavor, there are several ways it can be used. You can make *sangria,* a cold wine punch, by adding sugar or sugar syrup (to disguise the tartness of an opened or inexpensive red wine), a couple of slices of lemon and orange, and ice cubes. When you pour out the *sangria,* add a splash of soda water to give it zest. You can also make a spritzer from red or white wine by adding soda water—it's a refreshing aperitif. And finally you can make your own wine vinegar. Although wine that's been left out for a while will be attacked by the vinegar bacteria and will soon taste sour, it will not actually turn to vinegar by itself. You must add a quantity of vinegar to the leftover wine to start the process properly.

The amount of wine needed for a dinner will naturally vary, depending on the extent to which each of your guests enjoys wines. Even assuming that we are talking about people who normally drink wine with their meals, the amount of wine you should serve seems to vary in an almost geometrical proportion to the number of people present. Two people having a light supper may be happy to share a half bottle. Four people can easily drink two bottles, and six people at a big dinner might consume four bottles without any signs of overindulgence, especially if more than one kind of wine is served. The safest procedure is to have on hand—unopened—an extra bottle of whichever wine you're serving. Unfortunately, there are hosts who imagine that a single bottle of wine is adequate for six or eight people convivially gathered together, simply because no one clamors loudly for more wine. Such a host will have closed his eyes to the fact that all the glasses on the table have stood empty for most of the meal.

WINE AND FOOD

The question of which wine to serve with which food is one that seems to intimidate many, although perhaps not the lady who asked me if she could serve "white wine with everything, since red wine stains the tablecloth."* There are some who will invariably choose rosé as a happy compromise. There are times, of course, when a rosé is indeed the most appropriate choice: with a light luncheon, on a picnic, or in informal surroundings, its simple and refreshing qualities are perfectly in keeping with the mood of such occasions. But there is such a tremendous variety of red and white wines that are not only more interesting but also will more effectively set off a carefully prepared dish that it's a pity not to be more adventurous when choosing wines. It's perhaps well to recall here, without prejudice, that a rosé is technically an incompletely made red wine and will rarely have the depth of character or distinct personality of either a good red or white wine.

The established customs concerning the pairing of food and wine are simple and logical, but reaction to the very existence of these informal guidelines can be extreme. At one end are the gastronomic societies whose members are

---

* The most effective way of taking out a red wine stain seems to be to throw white wine on it. It sounds strange, but I have seen this work on carpets, embroidered tablecloths, and silk shirts.

so concerned that every wine must match perfectly the dish with which it is served that a special committee meets a few days before each gala dinner to taste its way critically through the entire menu and the accompanying wines. Then there are those who democratically maintain that any wine goes with any dish—if it pleases you. This attitude is perfectly acceptable if everyone shares your taste, but a little experimenting will soon convince most people that there are very sound reasons for the few general rules that most wine drinkers follow.

For one thing, there are some foods with which wine does not go very well. The vinegar in a salad will bring out the potential vinegar in wine, and for that reason the salad course is served separately in France, after the main course. Wine doesn't taste its best with eggs, although a light red wine might be served with something like a cheese omelet. Spicy foods overwhelm wine, and beer is the usual accompaniment for curries. If you prefer to serve wine with a pungent dish, choose a strongly flavored chilled white wine, such as an Alsatian Gewürztraminer or Sancerre from the Loire. One last negative rule is that, generally speaking, red wines do not taste right with fish. The oiliness of most fish seems to give red wine a somewhat bitter and unpleasant taste, and the refreshing quality of a chilled white wine is much more enjoyable.

With these few admonitions out of the way, the most practical rule to follow in choosing wines is, The richer the dish, the richer the wine. For example, shellfish can be accompanied by a light, dry white wine, such as Muscadet or Soave. Fish served with a rich sauce calls for a wine with more body and more flavor, such as a white Burgundy. Simply grilled meats are enhanced by light, delicate red wines, whereas game or rich stews might better be served with a full-bodied Burgundy or Rhône wine.

The common rule, White wine with white meat, red wine with red meat, is a good start, but there are any number of exceptions. For example, roast chicken is a perfect dish to set off a fine red Bordeaux, and many people will prefer a Valpolicella or Chianti with *veal scaloppine,* especially if it's made with a cheese and tomato sauce. Conversely, in the summertime you may prefer a chilled glass of dry white wine with cold meats.

If wine is used in the preparation of a dish, it's traditional to use the same kind of wine as an accompaniment. Thus, *coq au vin* usually calls for a red wine, whereas the version made in Alsace, *coq au Riesling,* will naturally be accompanied by a white wine. This example suggests another useful guideline—pairing of regional dishes with regional wines. A rich Italian pasta dish calls for Chianti, *boeuf bourguignon* for a Burgundy such as Gevrey-Chambertin or Pommard, an *entrecôte bordelaise* for a Saint-Emilion or Médoc. It's always more fun to experiment, guided by your own common sense, than to stick to a few correct but unimaginative rules.

So far we have been matching a dish with a wine, but for more elaborate dinners you may want to serve more than one wine. There is certainly nothing unusual or particularly fancy about serving two or three wines with a meal, and it can be more fun than serving two or three bottles of the same wine, especially when you have several enthusiastic wine drinkers at the dinner table. There are some traditional guidelines concerning the service of more than one wine: white before red, dry before sweet, young before old.

White before red simply conforms to the normal sequence of food, assuming you are having a light appetizer, or shellfish, or even a cooked fish dish, before a main dish of meat. Also, because red wines are usually richer and more complex than white wines, serving a dry white wine second would diminish its qualities by comparison. Dry before sweet is traditional because sweet foods spoil our taste buds (and our appetite) for the more delicate foods to follow (which is why dessert is served last). This rule supersedes the previous one in that a sweet white wine such as Sauternes or a German Auslese will be served with the dessert, and therefore after the red wine.

Young before old, and a corollary, light before full, simply indicates that the best wines are served last, to avoid a disappointing anticlimax. The idea of serving poorer wines as the meal progresses, because by that time no one will know the difference, conjures up the image of a group of sodden diners for whom all rules are irrelevant. It is traditional to work toward the finest wine, often served with a mild cheese course. For example, if you are serving two red Bordeaux, the older one, presumably more matured and distinguished, will be preceded by the younger wine. If you are serving a Beaujolais and a Pommard, the fuller Burgundy will follow the Beaujolais.

Champagne is often suggested as the one wine (along with rosé, I suppose) that can be served throughout a meal. Although this is a generous gesture and will be greeted with enthusiasm, Champagne does not complement all foods, and its taste may pall at the end of an evening. Without bubbles, Champagne would taste something like a Chablis, and you can readily see that there are many dishes with which Champagne may be inappropriate, especially full-flavored meats. One possibility is to serve Champagne as an aperitif before the meal. Another is to serve it with the dessert, but in that case choose an *Extra Dry* rather than the bone-dry *Brut*.

Cheese and wine are traditional partners, although a cheese course is not as common here as in Europe. Even restaurants of the highest caliber, for example, will rarely present a cheese tray that is adequate. At a dinner, a cheese course, which precedes the dessert, gives the host the opportunity of presenting his finest wine of the evening. If you decide to bring out a good bottle at this point, be sure that the cheeses are not too strong or the wine will be overwhelmed.

As a final suggestion, if you want to try more than one wine when there are only two or three of you, think of opening some half bottles.

Cooking with Wine

There is really no such thing as cooking wine, and it's a mistake to imagine that you can cook with a wine that you wouldn't want to drink. Most of the alcohol in wine will evaporate during cooking, and what's left is its flavor. It's not necessary to use Chambertin to make a *boeuf bourguignon* or a *coq au vin*, but if you try to economize by using an inferior bottle of wine, all of its defects will be concentrated in the sauce.

Furthermore, it's actually uneconomical to buy cheap wine for cooking. Say that an elaborate seafood dish calls for a spoonful or two of Sherry to heighten its flavor. A cook who runs out to buy a cheap bottle of Sherry will have spoiled several dollars worth of food and perhaps an hour or more of preparation with a dime's worth of wine. What's more, because the Sherry is too poor to drink, the spoonful of wine has, in fact, cost the full price of the bottle.

Red or white wine that is left over from a meal can usually be refrigerated and used for cooking within a day or two.

WINE IN RESTAURANTS

One of the pleasures of dining out in Europe is the opportunity to taste good wines inexpensively and without fuss. Wine making is so widespread in Europe, and particularly in France and Italy, that a bistro or inn almost anywhere will feature local wines, often served in carafes, and no more expensive than a bowl of soup or a dessert. Unfortunately, wine drinking in American restaurants is neither so easy nor so cheap. All too often restaurant lists are both unimaginative and expensive, and the service of wine ranges from the indifferent to the pretentious. Ideally, the service of wine should be both correct and unobtrusive, but the sad fact is that most waiters know less about wine than all but the least knowledgeable of their customers.

Most of the elements of service that apply in the home are equally valid in restaurants. There are some aspects of wine service, however, that are more relevant to restaurants, and these are reviewed here briefly. If you plan to have wine, ask for the wine list while you are looking at the menu, otherwise you may be subject to a long wait between the time you order your meal and the moment when a wine list is finally put into your hands. If you've ordered a good red wine, make sure that it is brought to the table and uncorked as soon as possible. This is not only to let the wine breathe, but also to avoid the possibility of a forgetful waiter opening the bottle only after he has served the dish that the wine was meant to accompany. Getting wine brought to the table in time is particularly important if you plan to have a bottle of white wine with the first course, which is often prepared ahead of time and brought to your table minutes after you've ordered it. Tell the waiter not to bring any food to the table until the white wine is uncorked and ready to be served.

On the subject of white wine, it should be chilled, of course, but not too cold. If a wine is placed in an ice bucket at the beginning of a meal, and then served with the main course, it may well be overchilled and have lost almost all its taste. Don't hesitate to take the bottle out of the cooler and stand it on the table. Keep in mind that restaurants invariably use ice buckets that are not deep enough for a bottle of wine, especially German or Alsatian wines. The easiest solution is to turn the bottle upside down for a moment before the first glass is poured: this may look odd, but the alternative is to drink the first two or three glasses of white wine at room temperature.

Red wines are usually served in wine baskets, but they are actually pointless as used in most restaurants. An older red wine lying on its side in the cellar will have thrown a deposit. Because it is not possible in a restaurant to stand the wine up for a couple of hours to let the sediment fall to the bottom of the bottle, the alternative is to move the bottle carefully, always on its side, from its bin to a wine basket, and then bring it to the table without disturbing the sediment. Ideally, the wine should be decanted at this point, or at any rate poured very carefully into large wine glasses. What actually happens four times out of five is that the waiter grabs the bottle any which way and carries it carelessly to the serving station. There he pops the bottle into a waiting basket and brings it to the table. To make the farce complete, some waiters insert a corkscrew by rotating the bottle in its basket.

When you've ordered a wine, the waiter or captain should always show you the bottle before he opens it to make sure the wine is exactly the one you ordered, and of the vintage specified on the wine list (or at any rate one acceptable to you). If it's a better-than-average wine that you've ordered, especially an older one, be sure that there is no more than the usual space between cork and wine: older wines sometimes develop too great an air space, and this may in turn affect the wine adversely. If you note too much ullage, as this is called, draw it to the waiter's attention by way of letting him know that you'll be on your guard against an oxydized or maderized wine.

After opening the bottle, the waiter may show you the cork, or even hand it to you. The idea is that the cork should be sound and should smell of wine, not of cork. You can give the cork a squeeze and a sniff if you want, but the wine in the glass is what's really important. The waiter will then pour some wine into the host's glass, so that he can determine whether or not it is defective in any way. If you happen to be eating your first course when the red wine is poured, don't try to judge the wine against smoked salmon, tomato salad, creamed herring, vichyssoise, or whatever may be in your mouth. Take a piece of bread first, or else tell the waiter that you'll taste the wine a little later, at your convenience. If a wine is defective in any way, it should naturally be sent back. Some restaurants will do this more gracefully than others. Even the most accommodating restaurateurs will privately complain, however, that most of the wine that is sent back is perfectly sound—either the customer was trying to show off, or he had made an uninformed choice and mistakenly expected the wine to have a different taste. Actually, corky wine is very rare and easily detected—it's a wine contaminated by a faulty cork, and tasting strongly of cork rather than wine.

Wine glasses are often too small, and those ubiquitous three- and four-ounce glasses are inappropriate not only because they don't permit a good wine to be swirled and sniffed, but also because using a small glass seems such a mean and unpleasant way of drinking wine. The simplest solution is to ask for empty water goblets and fill them only a third. You can expect six to eight glasses of wine from a bottle, depending on how generously the waiter pours. It's a pity to run out of wine halfway through a meal, and if a second bottle seems too much, an extra half bottle might be the answer.

Choosing a wine can be complicated by an assortment of dinner choices in a party of four or more. Rosé is one solution, but certainly not the best one, especially if fine food is being served. It's easy enough to order a half bottle each of red and white. Another possibility is to order a bottle of white and a half bottle of red. Everyone gets a glass of white wine with his first course, then those having fish as a main dish continue with white wine, those having meat go on to the red.

These general observations aside, the most important question is, Which wine to order? This will naturally depend on the kind of restaurant that you're in. In most American restaurants and steak houses, not much wine is drunk and the list will consequently be a small one and probably ill chosen. The service is uncertain, as is the condition of the cellar, so that the best bet is usually an American wine from a dependable firm. If you can get one of the premium California varietal wines, so much the better. These include Pinot Chardonnay, Pinot Blanc, and Riesling for the whites; Cabernet Sauvignon, Pinot Noir, and Zinfandel for the reds. A French Beaujolais would be fine, if it's of recent vintage (doubtful if the turnover of wines is slow).

Italian restaurants have the usual range of Chianti, Valpolicella, Bardolino, and among the white wines, Soave, Frascati, and Verdicchio. Because this choice is a relatively small one and a few brands dominate the market, you can soon discover which wines you enjoy most and expect to find them listed on almost every Italian wine list.

Other regional restaurants—Hungarian, Greek, German, Spanish—usually list a few wines from their respective countries, and these are worth trying, as they are relatively inexpensive and probably more knowledgeably chosen than the Beaujolais or Pommard that may also appear on such lists. If you choose an unfamiliar white wine, it's wise to check with the waiter to make sure it is as dry as you would like.

One of the most popular kinds of restaurants is the French bistro type; it may or may not have checkered tablecloths, but the wine list will be quite similar from one to the other. The red wines will include Beaujolais and perhaps a Pommard or Volnay from Burgundy, a Saint-Emilion and a Médoc from Bordeaux, and a Côtes du Rhône or Châteauneuf-du-Pape from the Rhône. Typically, the white wines would be Pouilly-Fuissé and Chablis from Burgundy; Bordeaux Blanc or Graves from Bordeaux; and perhaps a Muscadet or Pouilly-Fumé from the Loire Valley. These are all sound and pleasant wines, and any one you've enjoyed before can be ordered again. Because bistro wine lists are set up for maximum flexibility of buying and replacement, they rarely indicate vintages, and the

Burgundies will be anonymous as to their origins (shipper, wine grower, or importer). When the bottle comes to the table, make sure that the white wines and Beaujolais are of recent vintages; the other red wines can take more aging. If the Bordeaux list includes a château wine, this will probably be a better bet than the standard Bordeaux Rouge, Médoc, or Saint-Emilion, especially if it costs only a little more than the district wines.

Several cuts above the popular bistro-type restaurants are the very good French restaurants featuring *haute cuisine,* attentive service, and more complete wine lists. Such a list will include a good representation of red Bordeaux, several dry white Bordeaux from Graves, and two or more sweet Sauternes to accompany dessert. It will also include a number of red and white Burgundies, not only the village appellations such as Nuits-Saint-Georges, Pommard, Meursault, and Puligny-Montrachet, but also *premier* and *grand crû* wines from individual vineyards such as Clos de Vougeot, Chambertin, Echézeaux, Volnay Santenots, Meursault-Perrières, and Bâtard-Montrachet. There will also be a selection of Rhône wines, white wines from Alsace and the Loire Valley, and perhaps a few delicate and flowery German wines from the Moselle and Rhine. Faced with such a variety of choices, it is a mistake to order the least expensive wines, because the status of the restaurant (not to mention its overhead) demands that even the least expensive wine be sold for at least five or six dollars. Thus, the least expensive wines have the highest markup, and you will generally get much better value if you spend another dollar or two. It's also a mistake to order the most expensive wines, because you will rarely get your money's worth. Red wines from the most famous vineyards need several years to develop the qualities for which they are known, and few restaurants maintain stocks of any but the most current vintages.

If you are having a white wine first and a red wine with the main dish, the variety of a good restaurant list should encourage you to experiment with the fresh and attractive wines from Alsace and the Loire Valley. (Riesling and Sylvaner will be drier, Traminer more fruity; Muscadet, Pouilly-Fumé, and Sancerre are all crisp, dry wines and offer a change from Chablis and Pouilly-Fuissé). The light and refreshing German wines are becoming popular here as an accompaniment to the first course, and there are few more delightful ways of starting a meal. Wines made from extra-ripe grapes (labeled Spätlese and Auslese) may be a bit sweet for a first course.

There remains, in the hierarchy of restaurants, the very finest of the country, where the food is superb and wine list seemingly endless. It is in such places that the wine enthusiast can really enjoy himself, not only because the list offers such variety but also because he will find wines listed that are no longer available anywhere else and often at very fair prices.

A number of these establishments have *sommeliers*, or wine stewards, who are entirely responsible for the service of wine. The best of them are more interested in matching your choice of food with the proper wine than in "pushing" expensive wines, and they can be very helpful when they sense that a customer has a real interest in wines.

Of course, if you're not in the mood to study a wine list, a glass of the bar wine will give you pleasure without fuss. It won't be distinctive, but it's wine and it will make the meal more enjoyable.

Vintages

FOR SOME REASON, even people who are relatively unfamiliar with wines become pontifically self-assured when
it comes to discussing the best vintage years. Wine drinkers
in America seem to be abnormally vintage-conscious, and
often react with suspicion if offered a wine that does not
represent what they imagine to be a great year. It has always seemed to me that a wine's vintage is the last fact to
consider when deciding what to drink with dinner: the
primary consideration should be the kind of wine that
you would like. Often enough, its vintage will turn out to
be of little importance. After all, more than three-quarters
of all the wine produced in the world is meant to be consumed within a year of the harvest. We do get many of
the best wines of Europe, but even so, vintage years per se
are not the key to their enjoyment.

The importance given to vintages is of relatively recent
origin. For centuries new wines were poured into goblets
directly from the barrel. If bottles were used as an inter-
mediate step, they were loosely stoppered up with oil-
soaked rags or a wooden peg. In the eighteenth century,
when an effective cork made of bark first became generally
available, it was discovered that Port improved with a
certain amount of bottle age. In consequence, the Port
bottle evolved during the eighteenth century from a squat
shape to the kind of bottle that we see today. In effect,
there emerged the binnable bottle—a bottle that can be
stored on its side, thus keeping the cork wet and expanded,
and preventing air from entering the bottle and spoiling
the wine. It is probable that the first Bordeaux to be bottled and stored away was the Lafite-Rothschild 1797, and a
few bottles are still displayed today at the château. The effects of bottle age became so greatly admired that in the

second half of the nineteenth century, red Bordeaux was vinified in such a way as to maintain its qualities for forty or fifty years, and these wines were rarely drunk before they were twenty years old. This is still true today in the case of Vintage Port.

The concept of a vintage year or vintage wine is often misunderstood. A vintage, or harvest, occurs every fall in all of the world's vineyards (and every spring in the Southern Hemisphere). Thus, every wine that is not a blend of years has a vintage, represented by the year on its label. Obviously, every year is a vintage year, although some are better than others. Now, in the case of Port and Champagne, the wines of several years are traditionally blended together. When an exceptionally good summer results in better-than-average wines, a vintage year is declared by the shippers, and the resulting wine bears on its label the year in which the grapes were harvested. In all other wine-producing regions, the words *vintage year* have no special meaning.

There are a number of factors that make one vintage better than another in a particular region, but the most important is the amount of sunshine between the flowering of the vines in June and the harvest in late September. As grapes ripen in the sun, their natural acidity decreases and their sugar content increases. Ideally, the vintage takes place when the sugar/acid balance is in correct proportion. The wine will consequently have enough alcohol (from its sugar) to be stable, and enough acidity to be healthy and lively. Rainy summers result in immature grapes that produce less alcohol, more acidity, and less coloring matter in the skins for red wines. The wines are therefore weak, thin, tart, and pale. In general, there are more good vintages for white wines than for reds—within a given district—because color is not as important to their appearance, extra acidity does less harm to their taste, and they do not need the depth of flavor that is expected of red wines.

Apart from the weather during the summer, a vintage may be affected by poor weather during the flowering, which will diminish the final crop, or by brief hailstorms, which can destroy a vineyard's production at the last minute. Sudden frosts, which can kill the budding vines, are less of a danger now, as growers in northerly vineyards have started using modern outdoor heating equipment to protect their vines during cold spells.

Every few years the press declares that another vintage of the century has been produced. These stories perpetuate themselves with their own momentum, the public store of misinformation is increased, and undue importance is given to all the wines of these publicized vintages. It is axiomatic that a wine can not be judged before it is made, because rain during the picking or any other last-minute catastrophe can seriously affect the quality of the wine. Yet the earliest rumors about a great vintage often begin as early as July, much to the amusement of the growers, who promptly increase the prices they had planned to charge for their wines.

One of the most unfortunate results of the publicity given to certain fine vintages is that the public, anxious to buy these wines as soon as they appear, consumes the best wines of each vintage long before their prime. The wave of anticipation that accompanies a publicized vintage carries in its wake the disappointment that must inevitably occur when a good red wine is drunk too young. A fine Bordeaux or Burgundy will demonstrate its quality only with the passage of years, when it has fully matured. If you drink such a wine soon after it has been bottled, you can perceive only in rough outline the particular qualities that have made it sought after and expensive. Of all the comparative tastings that can be arranged, few are more instructive or surprising than to compare wine from the same vineyard, for example a classified Bordeaux château, in two good vintages, say 1966 and 1959. You will understand, as you taste the older wine, why certain wines are so expensive, and you will also realize that to drink expensive wines too young is pretty much a waste of money.

Vintage charts, with their numerical rating system, are useful as a rough guide to recent years. The system is too summary, however, to give more than an indication of the comparative overall reputation of those vintages. After all, not all the wines of a top-rated year were equally good, and conversely, certain vineyards may have produced excellent (and inexpensive) wines in a year rated only good or fair. To the extent that vintage charts focus attention on a few vintages, they are guilty of perpetuating the public's tendency to concern itself only with the best vintages.

The greatest fault of vintage charts, however, and of the vintage-conscious, is that they presume that good years exist in a kind of chronological vacuum, wherein time stands still. While it's true that all wines change during their life in the bottle, not all wines change for the better. The consideration of a vintage takes on a different dimension for wines whose virtues are charm, lightness, and fruit, than for wines characterized by tannin, depth of flavor, and a slowly developing bouquet. On most vintage charts a great year is great forever, a lesser year uninteresting from the start. But every wine has a life cycle of its own, based on soil and grape on the one hand, and the nature of the vintage on the other. Some wines are at their best when they are bottled, remain good for a year or two, and then decline rapidly. Others reach maturity only after a few years in bottle, maintain their excellence for several years, and then very gradually decline.

Age alone is no guarantee of quality, nor is a good vintage, in itself, a guarantee that the wine will be enjoyable today. If we compare red Bordeaux from the outstanding 1961 vintage with wines from the underrated 1960s, a vintage chart will always indicate that the 1961s are better. In fact, the lighter, quicker-maturing 1960s were more agreeable than the 1961s (and at half the price) for three or four years after they appeared. Then the slower-maturing 1961s began to come into their own, and they will continue to improve for years while the 1960s have pretty much faded away. Now, comparing the same superb 1961s with the highly rated 1966s, the best wines of these two excellent vintages will mature quite differently. The best 1961s will not reach their peak until the late 1970s, while the elegant and well-balanced 1966s will demonstrate their charm within seven or eight years of the vintage.

The question to ask concerning vintages is not simply, How good are the wines of this year? but just as relevantly, When should various wines of this vintage be drunk? Here are some general remarks concerning the relative importance of vintages for different categories of wine.

Many of the world's white wines are now bottled within months of the vintage to retain their fruit and charm. Such wines should naturally be consumed young, within three years of the harvest. Bigger-bodied white wines, such as those from Burgundy, are longer-lived and their flavor improves with bottle age, but be careful of dry white wines much more than five years old.

Sweet white wines will retain their qualities for a longer time: the Spätlese and Auslese wines from Germany and the wines of Sauternes and Barsac are the best-known examples.

Just about all rosés are best consumed young, and the vintage on the label is more useful as a guide to the wine's age than to how good it is.

A large proportion of the world's red wines can be consumed when they appear, and your only concern should be, as with most whites, to choose a fairly recent vintage. Red wines that benefit from some years of bottle age include the Cabernet Sauvignon wines of California, certain Italian wines such as Chianti Classico and those of the Piedmont, and the aged *reservas* of Spain's Rioja district. Looking for wines that are five or ten years old is more important here than trying to remember specific vintage years.

It is in the realm of red Bordeaux that the most attention must be paid to vintages, because most of the famous châteaux will bottle their wines in every vintage, for obvious commercial reasons. The importance of soil and proper vinification is such that a good vineyard can often produce attractive wine even in an off-year. These wines are naturally less expensive than those of famous vintages and are often good value for the consumer. Furthermore, since the best wines of the best years need time to develop their expensive qualities, off-years have traditionally fulfilled the role of providing readily drinkable and more affordable wines. It must be stated, however, that in recent years wines from famous Bordeaux vineyards have become so expensive even in lesser vintages that they no longer offer the values they once did. Furthermore, if there is one characteristic that poor vintages have in common it is that such wines are basically incomplete and short-lived.

A final observation about vintages: the years that are best known invariably correspond to the best vintages in

France. Good vintages in Germany do not parallel those of France and are in any case less frequent. Nor do vintages in more southerly vineyards, notably in Italy and France's Rhône Valley, correspond to those of Bordeaux and Burgundy.

A GUIDE
TO RECENT VINTAGES

Red Bordeaux

These are the wines that benefit most from bottle age in good vintages, and they are the longest-lived of all table wines.

1970. A large crop of very good wines was harvested throughout the region: the best of them will develop into one of the finest vintages since 1945.

1969. A wide choice of attractive wines distinguished more by their fruit and charm than by their longevity.

1968. Below average quality, perhaps better than 1963 and 1965. As always, some châteaux produced agreeable wines.

1967. An abundant crop of good wines. They are somewhat lighter than the 1966s, but they will be enjoyable and dependable for some years to come.

1966. Excellent wines with elegance, fine balance, and style: the best vintage since 1961, although more supple and therefore faster to mature. Probably the best vintage for present investment, especially the Médoc and Graves.

1965. Generally poor wines were made: some châteaux were good values at first, but they are already starting to decline.

1964. Very good wines were made, the best of which justify the early publicity given to this vintage. Quality varied from vineyard to vineyard, however, and in general the wines of Saint-Emilion and Pomerol were more successful than those of the Médoc.

1963. A poor year: as usual, a few châteaux produced pleasant wines, but even these are now aging fast.

1962. Underrated at first, these wines have developed very well and their firm, well-balanced style makes them the best older vintage still readily available (and affordable).

1961. Now considered the best vintage of the last twenty years—classic wines with exceptional depth. The best still need some years before they will be at their peak. Unfortunately, the crop was small and those wines still available are very expensive.

1960. Very pleasing light wines that were overlooked at first, falling as they did between the highly publicized 1959 and 1961 vintages. They are now fading and somewhat overpriced today.

1959. Not the vintage of the century, as they were originally described, but excellent wines that make very good drinking today. The combination of publicity and scarcity has now made these wines extremely expensive.

White Bordeaux

The sweet wines of Sauternes and Barsac have not had many successful vintages in the past decade, but the best of them will last considerably longer than the dry wines of Graves.

1970. *Dry:*   Well-made and attractive wines.

      Sweet: Wines of great quality were produced in Sauternes and Barsac: they will probably rank among the great vintages of the past twenty years.

1969. *Dry:*   Good wines with lively acidity.

      Sweet: Although little high-quality Sauternes and Barsac was made throughout the district, many properties were able to produce good wines.

1968. Neither dry nor sweet wines of any distinction were produced.

1967. *Dry:*   Very good wines were made.

      Sweet: The best Sauternes and Barsac since 1962: rich, luscious, and well-balanced.

1966. *Dry:* Good wines.

      Sweet: Conditions were not right for the noble rot and these wines are of only average quality. Certain châteaux, using their best barrels, produced attractive wines.

1965. Of little interest today for either dry or sweet wines.

1964. *Dry:* Good wines, all but the best châteaux now aging.

      Sweet: Some acceptable wines were made, but they generally lack the desired richness.

1963. Of no interest today.

1962, 1961, and 1959. The dry wines are generally too old, but really excellent Sauternes and Barsac were made in these three vintages, and fine examples from the best châteaux are still to be found today.

Red Burgundy

Beaujolais is best drunk young: 1970 and 1969 are the best recent vintages. The *grand cru* wines, such as Moulin-à-Vent, Brouilly, and Morgon are longer-lived than a Beaujolais or Beaujolais-Villages.

The following notes apply to the wines of the Côte de Nuits and the Côte de Beaune.

1970. An abundant crop of quite good wines, some equal to the 1969s, many somewhat softer in character.

1969. Remarkably good wines with great style and depth of flavor: one of the very best vintages of the decade.

1968. Unattractive wines, rarely seen here.

1967. Agreeable wines, varying between a few good wines from the Côte de Nuits to some rather light wines in the Côte de Beaune.

1966. An excellent vintage, which produced elegant, supple, and well-balanced wines: the best older vintage still generally available.

1965. Of little interest.

1964. Full-bodied wines of fine character—excellent wines that can still be found today.

1963. Of little interest.

1962. Very good wines were made, perhaps even better in Burgundy than in Bordeaux: no longer easy to find, but worth looking for.

1961. As in Bordeaux, splendid, long-lived wines that are unfortunately very scarce today.

1960. A few acceptable wines were made, but they have now faded away.

1959. A large crop of very good wine was made, but the best examples are now expensive and hard to find.

White Burgundy

1970. Excellent wines were made throughout Burgundy—including Pouilly-Fuissé and Chablis—with perhaps even more fruit and balance than the 1969s.

1969. Very good wines were produced in the Côte de Beaune, perhaps slightly less good than the reds. Chablis and Pouilly-Fuissé are also good (and very costly).

1968. Generally undistinguished wines, although some agreeable examples found their way here.

1967. Uneven in quality and quantity: Chablis and Pouilly-Fuissé are very good; Côte de Beaune wines are less consistent, although many good wines were produced.

1966. Excellent white wines were made throughout Burgundy, but they are already becoming scarce.

Of older vintages, 1962 and 1961 were outstanding, 1964 very good but somewhat uneven—only the very best bottles from the best vineyards will still have the style and finesse for which these vintages were originally noted.

The Loire Valley

The white wines of the Loire Valley—Muscadet, Pouilly-Fumé, Sancerre, Vouvray—are best consumed young: the excellent 1970 and 1969 vintages are the ones to look for, plus 1967 and 1966 for red wines, such as Chinon, Bourgueil, and Saumur de Champigny.

The Rhône Valley

Vintages here do not always correspond to those of the rest of France. White wines and rosés do not need bottle age, of course, and recent vintages for the red wines are as follows:

1970. One of the best vintages in recent years—excellent red wines were produced throughout the region.

1969. Many good wines were made, although they are perhaps less successful than in other parts of France.

1968. Only fair, and somewhat dull in style.

1967 and 1966 both produced very good, full-bodied wines that will continue to improve. Of older years, 1961 and 1962 are the best, with 1964 not quite as good.

Rhine and Moselle

1970. A very large crop of attractive wines was produced, with a limited amount of Spätlese and Auslese wines.

1969. On the average, a good year with fruit and style— the Moselles somewhat better than the Rhine wines. The vintage is similar to 1967 in quality, except that the Spätlese and Auslese wines are not on the same outstanding level.

1968. Useful commercial wines were made, but *Natur* wines of the big estates are without distinction.

1967. Quite good wines were produced everywhere, but the vintage is notable for the exceptional quality of its Spätlese and Auslese wines, which are the best since 1959.

1966. Very good wines were made across the board, perhaps the best general level of the past five years, although the higher grades of Spätlese and Auslese are not in the same class as those of 1967.

Of recent older vintages, only the outstanding 1964s are still worth seeking out, and even then only the longer-lasting Spätlese and Auslese wines from the finest vineyards and best producers.

Italy

Italian wines can be consumed when they arrive, and in any case vintages are not meant to be taken very seriously. Often enough, wines are blended from two or more vintages, none of which necessarily correspond to the year on the label. Even the best red wines may be refreshed with younger wines as they age in cask, so that the use of *Riserva* on a label is more an indication that the wine was specially selected for longer aging than that the wine is made up entirely of the named vintage. Certain Chiantis and the best red wines of the Piedmont—Barolo, Gattinara, Barbaresco—will certainly improve with bottle age.

California

The white wines, rosés, and most of the reds can be drunk without much attention to vintages, and in fact comparatively few California wines even bear a vintage year. The best red wines—especially the Cabernet Sauvignon—will certainly improve with a few years in bottle, and some of the wineries are now holding back part of their stocks until these wines have achieved maturity. Additional information about California vintages will be found on page 134.

PRONUNCIATION GUIDE

Abboccato	ah-bo-*kah*-toe
Alella	ah-*lay*-l'yah
Aligoté	ah-lee-go-tay
Aloxe-Corton	ah-lox cor-tawn
Amontillado	ah-mon-tee-yah-doe
Anjou	ahn-joo
Auslese	*ow*-slay-zuh
Auxey-Duresses	oak-say duh-ress
Barbera	bar-*bear*-ah
Bardolino	bar-doe-*lee*-no
Barolo	bar-*oh*-loe
Barsac	bar-sack
Batârd-Montrachet	bah-tar mon-rah-shay
Beaujolais	bo-jo-lay
Beaune	bone
Beerenauslese	*beer*-en-*ow*-slay-zuh
Bernkastel	bearn-castle
Blanc de Blancs	blahn duh blahn
Blanc Fumé	blahn foo-may
Bocksbeutel	box-boy-tell
Bodega	bo-*day*-gah
Bonnes Mares	bon mar
Bordeaux	bore-doe
Bourgogne	boor-*gon*-yuh
Brouilly	brew-yee
Brut	brute
Bual	boo-ahl
Cabernet	ca-bear-nay
Calvados	cahl-vah-dohss
Carruades	cah-roo-ahd
Cassis	cah-seece
Cave	cahv
Chablis	shah-blee
Chai	shay
Chambertin	shahm-bear-tan
Chambolle-Musigny	shahm-bol moo-seen-yee
Chardonnay	shahr-doe-nay
Chassagne-Montrachet	shah-sahnyuh mon-rah-shay

Chasselas	shass-lah
Château	shah-toe
Châteauneuf-du-Pape	shah-toe-nuff-doo-pahp
Chénas	shay-nah
Chenin Blanc	shay-nan blahn
Chiroubles	shee-roobl
Climat	clee-mah
Clos de Bèze	cloh duh behz
Clos de Vougeot	cloh duh voo-joh
Colheita	cul-*yay*-tah
Corbières	cor-b'yair
Corton	cor-tawn
Cosecha	co-*say*-chah
Côte de Beaune	coat duh bone
Côte de Brouilly	coat duh brew-yee
Côte Chalonnaise	coat shah-lo-nayz
Côte de Nuits	coat duh nwee
Côte d'Or	coat dor
Côtes du Rhône	coat doo rone
Côte Rotie	coat ro-tee
Crémant	creh-mahn
Crû	crew
Crû Classé	crew clah-say
Cuvaison	coo-vay-zohn
Cuvée	coo-vay
Dão	down
Douro	doo-roe
Echézeaux	eh-shay-zoh
Edelfäule	ay-del-foil
Egri Bikavér	egg-ree bee-ka-vair
Entre-Deux-Mers	ahn'tr-duh-mair
Estufa	esh-*too*-fah
Fass	fahss
Fendant	fahn-dahn
Fiaschi	fee-ahss-kee
Fino	*fee*-no
Fixin	fix-ahn
Fleurie	fluh-ree
Framboise	frahm-bwahz
Frascati	frahss-*ca*-tee

Freisa	fray-zah
Frizzante	free-*zahn*-tay
Fuder	foo-duh
Gamay	gam-may
Gevrey-Chambertin	jev-ray shahm-bear-tan
Gewächs	guh-*vex*
Gewürztraminer	guh-*vurtz*-trah-*mee*-ner
Grands Echézeaux	grahnz eh-shay-zoh
Graves	grahv
Grenache	greh-nahsh
Gumpoldskirchen	goom-poles-*kir*-ken
Haut	oh
Hermitage	air-mee-tahj
Hospices de Beaune	oh-speece duh bone
Jerez	hair-reth
Johannisberg	yoh-*hah*-niss-bairg
Juliénas	jool-yeh-nah
Kirsch	keersh
Lacrima Christi	*la*-cree-mah *kriss*-tee
Lascombes	lass-comb
Mâcon	mah-kohn
Maderisé	mah-dair-ree-zay
Malmsey	*mahlm*-zee
Manzanilla	man-zah-*nee*-ya
Marc	mar
Margaux	mahr-go
Médoc	meh-dock
Merlot	mehr-loh
Meursault	muhr-soe
Mise en bouteilles	meez ahn boo-tay
Montrachet	mon-rah-shay
Morey-Saint-Denis	moh-ray san-deh-nee
Morgon	mohr-gohn
Moulin-à-Vent	moo-lahn-ah-vahn
Mousseux	moo-suh
Muscadet	muhss-ka-day
Musigny	moo-see-nyee
Nahe	nah
Naturrein	nah-toor-rine

Neuchâtel	nuh-shah-tell
Nierstein	neer-shtine
Nuits-Saint-Georges	nwee-san-jawrj
Oloroso	oh-lo-ro-so
Originalabfüllung	oh-*rig*-ee-nahl-*ahb*-fuh-lung
Orvieto	ohr-vee-*ay*-toe
Pauillac	paw-yack
Pays	pay-yee
Pétillant	pet-tee-yahn
Petit	puh-tee
Phylloxera	fil-*lox*-uh-rah
Pinot Noir	pee-noe nwahr
Poire	pwahr
Pomerol	pom-uh-rohl
Pommard	poh-mar
Pouilly-Fuissé	poo-yee fwee-say
Pouilly-Fumé	poo-yee foo-may
Pourriture noble	poo-ree-toor nohbl
Premier Crû	preh-m'yay crew
Puligny-Montrachet	poo-lee-nyee mon-rah-shay
Puttonys	puh-tohn-yosh
Recioto	ray-*tshot*-oh
Retsina	ret-*see*-nah
Rheingau	rine-gow
Rheinhessen	rine-hessen
Rheinpfalz	rine-faltz
Richebourg	reesh-boor
Riesling	*reece*-ling
Rioja	ree-*oh*-ha
Rosé	roh-zay
Ruwer	*roo*-vuh
Saar	sahr
Sancerre	sahn-sair
Sauternes	saw-tairn
Sauvignon Blanc	saw-vee-yohn blahn
Secco	say-co
Sekt	sekt
Sémillon	seh-mee-yohn
Soave	so-*ah*-vay
Solera	so-*lair*-ah

Sommelier	so-mel-yay
Spätlese	shpaht-lay-zuh
Spumante	spoo-*mahn*-tay
Sylvaner	sil-*vah*-ner, sil-vah-*nair*
Tastevin	taht-van
Tavel	tah-vell
Terroir	tehr-wahr
Tête de Cuvée	teht duh koo-vay
Tonneau	tun-oh
Traminer	trah-*mee*-ner, trah-mee-*nair*
Tröckenbeerenauslese	*trok*-en-*beer*-en-*ow*-slay-zuh
Valdepeñas	val-day-*pain*-yass
Valpolicella	val-poh-lee-*t'chell*-ah
Vaud	voh
Verdelho	vehr-*dell*-yoh
Verdicchio	vehr-*dee*-kee-oh
Vinho Verde	*veen*-yoh *vair*-day
Vinifera	vin-*if*-uh-rah
Vin ordinaire	van or-dee-nair
Vosne-Romanée	vohn ro-mah-nay
Vougeot	voo-joh
Yquem	ee-kem

Index

INDEX

BIOGRAPHY

Alexis Bespaloff spent his earliest years in Belgium and Brazil before coming to New York City, and was educated at Amherst College and Harvard University. He worked for two years in Bordeaux as director of a wine buying and shipping office for an American importer, and has been more recently associated with the Alexis Lichine Company in New York. He has contributed articles to a number of British and American publications, was retained as wine consultant by Time-Life Books, and is currently at work on two more wine books. In addition to several wine buying trips throughout France, he has visited the vineyards of Germany, Italy, Spain and Portugal, as well as those of New York State and California.

SIGNET Books for Your Reference Shelf

☐ **THE SIGNET ENCYCLOPEDIA OF WINE by E. Frank Henriques.** The complete guide to brand names, vineyards, vintages, varieties and labels of over 20,000 wines. Here is a book that defines, interprets and translates every prominent word on any wine label—a book you can use for profit and pleasure your whole wine-drinking life. (#E6751—$2.25)

☐ **INEXPENSIVE WINE: A Guide to Best Buys by Susan Lee.** If you've ever felt lost amid the bewildering array of labels at your local wineshop, then this is the book for you. Here is a book that will help you separate the real bargains from the rip-offs. With over 400 wines rated, this is the best investment you can make in your quest for good but low-priced wine. (#W6680—$1.50)

☐ **THE SIGNET BOOK OF AMERICAN WINE by Peter Quimme.** Complete. Authoritative. Practical. Everything you need to know to buy, evaluate, and enjoy all the different wines of America. The indispensable companion volume to **The Signet Book of Wine.** (#W6464—$1.50)

☐ **COOKING WITH WINE by Morrison Wood.** The best of the world's most famous foods can now be prepared in your own kitchen. An expert shows how available ingredients are transformed into exotic fare by the creative use of American wines and liqueurs. (#Y6577—$1.25)